629.283
K386c

D0287037

CRASH!

What You Don't Know About Driving Can Kill You!

Lincoln Branch Library
1221 E. Seven Mile Road
Detroit, Michigan 48203
313-481-1782

by
Dr. Lauren Kennedy-Smith

MAR 2013

LI

Copyright © 2012
Dr. Lauren Kennedy-Smith
and Dr. Lauren Innovations
First Edition — August 2012
www.drlaurenspeaks.com

ISBN
978-1-4602-0203-6 (Paperback)
978-1-4602-0205-0 (eBook)

All rights reserved. No part or page of this publication can be copied or quoted in any form, materially or electronically without the expressed, written permission of Dr. Lauren Kennedy-Smith or her official representatives.

Published by:

FriesenPress

Suite 300 — 852 Fort Street
Victoria, BC, Canada V8W 1H8

www.friesenpress.com

Distributed to the trade by The Ingram Book Company.

This publication is endorsed by Better World Initiatives (BWI), a multidisciplinary organization of global contributors dedicated to positive human growth through local, national and international educational products, projects and events.

Table of Contents

For Matt

Acknowledgments

I want to thank those of you who understood from the beginning why I chose and became determined to write a book about what have been, until now, ignored but critical aspects of driving. Alison's early, alighting enthusiasm was very helpful. Dr. Brent Kay nudged and pushed me when I fell back to attend to a million other matters. Liam and Rainn T. handled research files knowing I'd lose them and Dr. Flora and her wonder nurse, Colleen, continue to help me handle rough days amid a hectic schedule. They're great! Thanks to Eva and Dan for corralling the drivers who were gently coerced into reading the manuscript and then driving and reporting back about changes in their insights and driving patterns. Thank you to OPP officers and Massachusetts state troopers for their harrowing stories and shared worry about manic, erratic and unfocused driving. Be thankful when they pull you over for driving at risk. Thank you to Jane Ginsberg for handling office and other matters as this book turned into a larger than expected commitment of time and energy. Heartfelt thanks to my "One Dog" Hunter for forcing me to take breaks and to join her in amiable silence on nearby nature trails. I remain grateful to Betty Harrison for knowing that when I seem to have vanished, I am, more often than not, writing. Know that I continue to fight the good fight. Much thanks to Pearl Graham for taking on a short editing task mid-way through. Sue and Steven Clark, Dan Waters, and Kevin Drysdale, thank you for running the focus groups and keeping the catering bill down. To Michael Keen, President of Opinionation Inc., an international research and polling company, thank you for your inspiration and for the ongoing, international credibility of your focus group software. To Lorraine Greenwood, makeup specialist extraordinaire in Toronto television circles, thank you for your kindness to all and for your heroic efforts to tame my hair and maintain my "face base" in the 95 degree heat of 14 hour production days. To LLL, much thanks for company among night owls by a lake—and for the time I shared with Chloe and Sophie. Thanks to Shari for her efforts during the final stages of this book. It's my bet she's a good driver. Much gratitude to Dr. L. Puil for her interest in and support for this project. Lastly, thank you to Dyan McCann for planning the first launch. Thank you, Helen, for the genetic gift of persistence and to Kyle, Luke and Jake for eventually understanding the unnecessarily complex web adults can weave. Stay safe.

A NOTE TO THE READER
How to Use this Book

In order to absorb and use the life and limb saving information in this book, I advise the reader to approach it as an experience. As information is taken in, new thoughts and insights will inevitably form. Your driving will change almost immediately.

First, however, if the reader has any anxiety at all about improving his or her driving, use positive visualizations—or mental pictures—to eliminate anything resembling fear. If anxiety arises while going through the book, stop, take a deep breath, and know that you can learn here in private, and at your own pace.

One of the reasons for completing this book is related to an experience in which I observed a number of anxious and defeated drivers, strangers to each other and to their instructors, come together with the hope of improving their driving. For each driver, unlearning old and dangerous habits was an urgent matter, one that would make a significant improvement to his or her life. There was no room for failure. However, the success rate for most, once the candidates and adult students returned home from their lessons, was no doubt limited—and this was primarily due to the fact that they approached their activities from a place of low self-esteem and high anxiety. The latter emotion—a form of fear—is the precursor to, and the fuel for both low self-esteem and sundry defeating emotions.

Regardless of how lessons or information are structured and who is teaching and how, no one can learn anything when he or she is fearful—and this includes anxiety, nervousness, fatalistic doubt and more. When we are fearful, whether we are driving or participating in other life activities, we are both ineffective and prone to errors in judgment and actions. Furthermore, we can be shown a task a hundred times and have it explained repeatedly but still not "get" it when our thinking and computing abilities are blocked by the most toxic of human emotions. Do everything you can—gently—to proceed with positive enthusiasm in reading this book.

Retention and Structure

Studies show that the North American reading retention level—directly related to our ability to concentrate—is way down. Therefore, the best way to approach the vital information in these pages is to personalize the process, to tailor it to your time constraints and reading habits, as well as to what you suspect might be your specific driving weaknesses.

The book is organized in such a way so as to encourage the reader to review new concepts before moving on to the next section. This approach and format is critical to a book that presents a number of concepts and facts about driving never before entertained by the vast majority of drivers.

The reader should spend more time on or re-read chapters in which he or she finds particularly pertinent and new information both as it relates to driving in general, and as it relates to his or her driving concerns.

New and more experienced drivers might very well approach CRASH! differently. There are suggestions in the appendix that address these differences. Relatedly, all drivers should, ideally, get to a point where they share what they have learned and discuss it with others. However, for novice drivers in particular, after they have read at their own pace and returned to re-examine certain issues and chapters, it is useful to discuss new insights with peers as well as with seasoned drivers. We can all improve our driving with increased understanding and discussion, and we can all make life and death differences by doing so. However, new drivers can launch an era and standard of "sane" driving that has never before existed.

So, first, make reading this book a personal experience, not a "must do" assignment, with a time limit and one on which there will be tests and pass or fail consequences. The constraints have been eliminated for a reason—they get in the way of learning, and the absorption and practical application of new knowledge. More experienced and older drivers are well-advised to take a similar, personalized approach. It is urgent that the information in these pages be acquired and adopted by as many drivers as possible. This is precisely why the book should be approached as an individualized learning experience. I dare say, it can also be enjoyable and, in some places, entertaining.

One last suggestion. Have a highlighter on hand, especially for the first three chapters of the book. These chapters lay the "theoretical" or explanatory groundwork for the "get your teeth into" chapters to come. Furthermore, there are helpful reviews at the end of each chapter and I am willing to bet that what you underline will come up, in some way, in the questions.

As a longtime pedagogue or formal teacher of all things performance related, including high-speed driving, it is my intent and hope that you, the reader, will come to own this book and make it into a personal, driving workbook. Use the space between the questions to note answers and queries. Write reminders and various matters to be discussed with others in the notes section at the end of each chapter. Well-read books, from which much is learned, are messy after the fact. So, go ahead and also add notes in the margins, underline, highlight and re-think, reflect and re-read where the information hits a personal note. Also as a teacher and a mental health professional, I again urge and remind the reader to dispose of all anxiety related to perceived driving inadequacies and needs, as well as to any unfounded illusions about an inability to learn. Open your mind and adopt a positive posture. It is astounding what one can learn with an open mind and "no fear".

Dr. Lauren
Cape Cod, 2012

CRASH!

CHAPTER ONE
Know Where You Are Going— and How

I can drive with my eyes closed. Always could. Except when I'm putting on my makeup. Then I like to see what I'm doing.

Maggie T.

Do you know how to drive? The vast majority of us think we are good drivers. Furthermore, driving is treated as if it is as commonplace and as simple as eating fast food or drinking coffee. Driving may be commonplace but it is most certainly not simple.

If we are all such fundamentally good drivers, why do so many drivers and passengers die each year on our roads and highways? Why is there so much "conflict driving", and why are there so many accidents, the causes of which are rarely, if ever, mechanical, related to the weather or due to the dubious construction and grade of a highway? This book will answer these questions in a way that will be new to both the beginning and the experienced driver—and, the author trusts, neither will ever view driving the same way again.[1]

According to professional drivers—NASCAR drivers, stock car racers, police officers, long-time licensed chauffeurs, award-winning cab drivers and others—the vast majority of drivers on the roads today are profoundly limited at the wheel. This does not mean that most drivers lack the intelligence or ability to master the basic technical skills. Rather, the limitation refers to the fact that most people wield vehicles with little, if any, awareness of what is going on around them and with no real insight into the potential for catastrophe. In addition, the vast majority drive with inadequate focus and the wrong kind of focus. Focusing on one's signaling, steering, braking, and other basics learned in driving courses is standard. But it is not enough. A wider and more personal focus and level of awareness is required for safe, let alone for good, defensive, intelligent driving.

In the pages to come, the reader will learn what is required to claim excellence and responsibility as a driver on modern roads and highways. With the information and discussion in this book, both the new and experienced driver will

---

1   Drivers in a pilot study, who were asked to read this manuscript and then drive normally for two weeks, reported significant changes in their driving behavior.

be able to re-think the driving process. He[2] will become a better driver by absorbing and then incorporating never-before-presented aspects of driving into his own experience. With approximately 75% of serious accidents attributed to distractions or inattention of one kind or another, clearly we need to learn a new way to focus at the wheel.[3]

Focused Awareness

The predominating aspects of safe, smart driving are focused awareness and conscious awareness. Focused awareness refers to our being aware of and committed to focusing on everything that is going on around us (and our vehicle). It includes an awareness of what is happening within our vehicle in terms of movements and distractions. Conscious awareness refers to the need to be aware of, and conscious of, our reactions and behavioral inclinations at the wheel. This overlapping, two-fold focus is both the crux and the challenge of mindful and responsible driving.

2   "He" and "she" are used interchangeably throughout the book. I deliberately switch back and forth in order to avoid any inference about whether women or men are good, better or worse at a particular aspect of driving. This is because most of the popular assumptions about genders and driving are myths. However, when there is some evidence that a behavior or action is more likely to be performed by one gender, I have so indicated.

3   See Distraction.gov, the Official U.S. Government Website for Distracted Driving, the U.S. Department of Transportation National Highway Traffic Safety Administration, http://www.dis-traction.gov/content/get-the-facts/research.html.

Destination

Focused awareness also refers to and must incorporate the critical requirement that, as drivers, we must always know exactly where we are going and why. This seems obvious. However, as we will see later in the book, a sense of destination is a "balancer" when things get tough. It keeps us focused in the moment on our route, instead of on the vagaries of the car in front of us, and it is a conscious and unconscious reminder of the where, why and importance of our arrival. No matter what is going on around us, a sense of destination forces us to keep our mind's eye on our route.

Driving as Socializing

Still under the umbrella of focused and conscious awareness, we will look at the fact that, when we drive, we move (albeit somewhat encased) among strangers with whom we are intimately entwined, and we do so at high speeds in a restricted space. In addition, we are, on a general if usually unspoken level, pitted against each other in a strange kind of cultural competition, based fundamentally on speed, position and the identifying value of the car we drive. However, even aside from the competitive aspects of North American driving, it is of the utmost importance that we recognize and address the fact that driving is a charged social activity. It is, in fact, an *interactive* process, something we fail to address or to admit due to the illusion of privacy we have ascribed to being in our cars. Coming to terms with, and incorporating the social aspect of driving into our current driving perspectives and patterns, is the best and most fundamental way to begin the process of ensuring that our own driving is safe and sound. Further to the dual principle of focused and conscious awareness, the information in this book gives the reader a way to think about and determine what she brings to traffic in the way of odd, extreme, or just distracting postures and moods. It will also bring our attention to how dangerous it is to be casual about who we take on as passengers. We can invite distractions into our most personal driving space and thus affect the wider "people environment". By driving with problematic friends, relatives, or even spouses by our side, we increase the chances for personal distraction. Passengers commonly push drivers' buttons—and not uncommonly, they push them right off the road or into another car. Importantly, this book includes a short section on what is at the root of traffic conflict. Drivers are more than just strange, limited creatures driving monstrously dangerous four-wheeled land projectiles. We are each a mix of differences and similarities, of differing perspectives and often contradictory driving agendas. And when the pressure is on, drivers can do almost anything.

To remain cool, calm and non-reactive in the face of, for example, a deliberate cut-off and close call requires more than steering and braking skill. Self-awareness and self-discipline are critical to what happens next. Too many accidents happen when drivers are either reacting or offending with a rush of adrenaline. Real or perceived slights can bring an ugly end to even the loveliest summer drive. In fact, however, slights and other basic distractions should be made irrelevant by a few key factors, not the least of which is our commitment to the process of reaching our destination.

An entire chapter is devoted to focus and awareness so that the reader can absorb and compute some of the crucial elements of self-conscious driving.[4] The emphasis on destination will further highlight the fact that we have to do more than just arbitrarily head out for a drive. We need to adopt what could be described as a macro and a micro sense of our destination and our trip to get there. Our commitment to focusing on where we are ultimately headed is a way of maintaining and checking in on our focus in any moment. It is also a way to avoid following a wayward car going in a dangerous direction, and to sustain a safe level of uninterrupted focus.

The above represents the general concepts that will be broken down and personalized in what is to come. As concepts are looked at in more detail, the driver-reader will start to identify and to pick and choose in relation to what fits and makes personal sense, and what does not.

I dare suspect that some readers have already had a sense of something personal—and especially useful—to come.

---

4   "Self-conscious" means being conscious of one's self and emotions at any given time.

CHAPTER ONE: Review

1. Do you imagine that you would want to be friends with every other driver on the road? Why or why not?

2. Why are other drivers who share the road with you relevant to your driving?

3. When you first started driving, did you care what kind of car you drove? Do you care now? Why?

4. What do you generally do when someone picks a fight? Join in? Or, move away? Why is this relevant to driving?

5. Why might idle driving to nowhere be more dangerous than having a destination?

6. What is road rage? Think of an example of how it may occur.

7. What driving habits or behaviors do you have that you would not want others to see?

Notes

Notes

CHAPTER TWO
Modern Driving and the Primitive Mind

If I could just drive by myself, I'd be fine. Others just make every-thing more difficult and nerve-wracking. I don't trust anyone to be as careful as I am.

Elaine, Engineering Student

In western society, we like our space. We also like to have control over our environments, over who we spend time with, for how long, and when. Depending on our personality type, being forced to spend time with medium to large groups of strangers can be experienced as anything from unpleasant to inducing of a full blown anxiety attack. To varying degrees, this pertains to all human beings, not just those in the western world. Crowds, for example, tend to scare us because of the sheer number of *other* people and their *unfamiliarity*. We need our small, "tribal" connections in order to be mentally healthy.

Our preference for small groups and for familiarity also plays out when we drive. This is an element of driving that has received too little, if any, attention as new drivers are introduced to the driving landscape. We are "crowd averse" wherever we are and whatever we are doing. This is just how we are wired and have been since our ancestors inhabited the primitive village. In spite of our ability to build multi-lane super-highways, elongated tunnels and five-mile-long bridges constructed to accommodate more and more vehicles, we are all still at a neurological (and, therefore, social) developmental stage better suited to the horse and buggy.

Our ideal state is one in which we share tasks, duties and recreation with a familiar handful of people. It is in this particular context of safety that we are able to develop and hone skills, to be healthily alert, and to perform from a core of well-being. Without this mental and emotional "safe space", we are distinctly less competent at everything we do and infinitely less likely to connect with and understand others.

Driving Unaware

It is important to emphasize that it is news for most that when we drive, we are performing a task for which we are not sufficiently developed. Needless to say, the implications for modern driving are both serious and warranting of some urgent instruction and re-education. As we will see more and more as we go through this book, virtually everything we do when we are driving is interactive or *social*—and performed in a crowded, unfamiliar, human environment with no alternative other than opting out of a driving or car culture.

At this point, very few drivers (and readers) will fully comprehend or accept the notion and reality that we are fundamentally "off" or going against the essence of our development when we drive. When asked, drivers speak in very blunt and simple terms about both their driving and their cars or trucks. Most if not all drivers covet time alone in their vehicles, tasking and zooming from point A to a rough point B, sometimes coasting, playing music, and basically kicking back before arriving at a destination where they have to face adult or near-adult responsibilities. Driving, in spite of the inanely huge stock we place in what we drive and how we might be perceived in relation to our vehicle, is generally viewed and approached as a mere task to be performed without much thought. As significant a role as it plays in most North Americans' lives, it is given the attention of something that is a means to an end, a sidebar to the real narrative that is our lives. Yet, as we will see, how we view or measure ourselves as drivers is a key aspect of our sense of who we are. Criticism aimed at our driving prowess is, as most readers would agree, almost unendurable. And it can spark a level of defensiveness and drama that can shock even the most self-aware of individuals.

Our Cars—Almost Like Home

We hold many sentiments about our cars and they are often contradictory or not based in the reality of the structure of the modern vehicle. We have all left a meeting, social event, or class and searched for our cars in large parking lots, or worse, parking garages. We have further experienced the overwhelming relief of finally locating our cars and climbing in, locking the doors, taking a quick look around and breathing a clandestine sigh of enormous relief. Our cars are places in which we deem ourselves to be alone and virtually invisible. They are spaces in which we can have a hiatus from fitting in, looking good or having to be "on" and agreeable among other people. We have long perceived our cars—whether they are moving or not—as mobile nests and hiding places with all the benefits of cozy privacy. Far from seeing cars as instruments of social engagement, we experience our cars as exquisitely private spaces in which we can yell, pursue a loud and profane argument with someone not present and freely relieve digestive pressure. In that our cars are virtually private, soundproof dens on wheels, it is of little wonder why we are so emotionally invested in them.

Concrete Illusions

However, whether we are moving or are stopped at an intersection, we are under a comfortable illusion. We suffer a kind of denial with respect to how private or how social the task of driving (and being in our cars) actually is. While we notice the occupant of the car next to us performing a visceral nasal clean-up, we do so from our own presumption of privacy and at least quasi-invisibility. This odd contradiction in perception contributes to a singular kind of perceptual misalignment and causes all kinds of mishaps on our roads and highways. As humans, we act differently when we think or *feel* that we cannot be seen. In order to strengthen the illusion, we avoid eye contact when normally flowing traffic slows down or when we are at stoplights. We work to reinforce an anonymity that, in fact, doesn't exist. For example, for some drivers it is fine if another driver sees a rude hand gesture but not the gesturer's face—even though all one has to do is check a license plate to put a name and address to the messenger. Our favored tinted windows, once commonly and deliberately darker and more concealing than the new legal standard, have caused problems for police forces. Laws had to be passed so that police could see in and to ensure that we could see out—at least to determine whether it was day or night. Tints help us to conceal ourselves and to *feel* hidden. It is both symbolic and one of the tangible means we use to hide, to be left alone in traffic, and to shirk our responsibility for how we behave among others in the social context of traffic. But we cannot hide and drive at the same time, even if the illusion of being safe and out-of-view arises from a very real, primitive, and overriding need.

Task Behavior, Driving and the Primitive Village

Not so long ago, human beings lived in very small groups, with narrowly defined responsibilities or tasks. As most of us learned in our early history courses, in the primitive village there were those who hunted, those who cooked, raised children, and others who gathered wood for fire or materials to build and reinforce dwellings. These life-sustaining activities went on year after year and generation after generation. Each person knew what was expected of him or her and each knew what was expected from and predictable about others in the village family. Life was not without its dangers and hardships but for the most part, the activities and tasks related to daily life were carried out with a consistency that comes with familiarity and a critical sense of safety. Life within the village held few surprises—and this was the point.

Troubles began with the increasing arrival and passing through of strangers. As populations in what had been isolated areas grew, villages and villagers were, for the first time, threatened. Villagers, to whom everyone had once been related and familiar, trustworthy, predictable and supportive, were both shaken and frightened by the near and unpredictable presence of new people. Though daily tasks and routines continued, everyone grew more vigilant and the hunters began to have to think and strategize about protecting the village.

Soon, there was interaction among villages and groups of villages that included conflict, some negotiation, and some trading. In time, there was some mutually cautious protection, as well. However, as anthropologists have learned, basic aspects of daily life such as skinning the spoils of the hunt or cooking continued to involve a maximum of five people at a time. And, more often, basic tasks were commonly carried out by three familiar village members. Even more significant when it comes to a related and critical aspect of driving is the fact that, as man and womankind evolved and life became both more complex and more labor-intensive, human beings remained inclined, by instinct and necessity, to perform life tasks and larger endeavors in small, known, trusted and predictable groups. If forced out of this comfort zone, they were unable to function. This fundamental aspect of human development, behavior, interaction and collaboration has never changed.[5]

Still Primitive After All These Years

Needless to say, inhabitants in primitive times did not travel very far to perform their duties. However, had *it become mandatory* that villagers and family members leave the familiar security of their units each day and travel

---

5   Many corporate managers appear to be unaware of this principle
     when they assign groups or divisions to a project.

among complete strangers to various destinations, they would soon have been afflicted with pervasive mental disorders. Studies have shown that much that afflicts modern man and woman arises out of both the speed and the "disconnect" (detachment from others) inherent in daily life. As humans, we thrive in small, familiar units and become discernibly "unwell" and out-of-balance if we cannot find a way to simulate familiar units in large crowded cities. With the industrial revolution, and the sprawl and overcrowding of urban metropolises, large populations began to suffer from the disintegration of the "village-like" social unit. Depression, anxiety, confusion, addictions and other ailments related to the dilution of a sense of "belonging" and from too little meaningful human contact became facts of "modern" life. Had primitive villagers been forced, in a generation, to live and work among thousands (even just hundreds) of strangers, humankind might very well have gone the way of the dinosaur. We adapted remarkably, but we did not, in fact, change, nor could we speed up our development or undergo a miracle mutation to prepare us for the arguable insanity to come.

For us now, as both urban (and rural) dwellers and drivers, very little has changed psychologically. Neurologically we are stuck in primitive patterns and with primitive needs. Our fundamental need for familiarity and community—in all that we do—is as strong as ever. Regardless of social and structural changes, from honeycomb high rises to multi-lane highways, the latter built precisely for the efficient overcrowding of high-speed vehicles driven poorly by strangers, we cope. However, in the end, where movement, mechanics, crowds and the need to self-protect, to hide and to seek privacy are concerned, we have not adapted. Nor will we. The part of our brain that compels us to connection, intimacy, and love in small and familiar groups has stood firm against time, social proliferation, overpopulation and technological absurdity. The same section of the brain (actually referred to as "the primitive brain") that was and *is* at work to protect us from danger, stayed at its post.[6] And it has a problem with us driving. Thus the origin of the suppressed or conscious discomfort mere mortals naturally bring to the unpredictable, high-speed chaos of traffic.

Driving Among Strangers

Regardless of the fact that we remain neurological slaves to the "three to five rule", we have had to develop ways to form and tolerate collaborations in *most* aspects of modern life. However, where driving is concerned, we have been unable to do so. We bring what is for most of us an unconscious discomfort, a form of anxiety, to the social context that is driving. Regardless of where we are headed in a car, we are performing a complex task, at dangerous speeds, among and amid a horde of strangers. In short, we engage in a multidimensional and overstimulating process for which our brains are underdeveloped. Before we can face the notion of being scrunched among other discomfited strangers, we are, by virtue of development and instinct, functioning with diminished capacity.

Strangers Driving Among Strangers—The Crux

Understanding that driving is a distinctly unnatural and, therefore, an innately awkward and perilous social activity

---

6   One of the structures in the primitive portion of our brains is called the amygdala—a small almond shape more or less at the center of the primitive part of the brain. It is vital to aspects of social behavior.

is just the beginning. Regardless of the fact that we still have a primitive need to perform among a few familiar and trusted people, most of us have to drive in actual traffic. We also have to periodically perform other tasks among too many people or, to be more specific, among more people than with whom we are fundamentally comfortable. As is the case in work and other life situations, in the context of driving, there is much more that we can do to increase our comfort level than merely super-tint our windows and refuse to look sideways. A significant step toward a shift in perception and improved performance (and safer driving) would be to acknowledge, accept and address the fact of our unconscious or conscious anxiety. If we then take another leap from the confines of our artificial solitude and recognize that we all drive as individuals with fears, different personalities and perspectives, preferences, habits and more, we begin to shed light on the most critical and dangerous aspects of driving. Not only are we fundamentally uncomfortable zooming our way around and throughout our lives, but we are also bound to compensate for our discomfort. We each bring our individual habitual ways of performing other tasks or activities to driving, and our approaches are exaggerated as we struggle and strain for some degree of control, as well as for a sense of predictability and safety.

Essential to the purpose of this book is the reader's commitment to thinking about the fact that we are all ill-equipped to perform the task of driving among others with *consistent* competence. We cannot be competent and precise when we are consciously or unconsciously anxious. This realization and understanding is the first major step toward achieving both conscious awareness and focused awareness, that is, the honing and sustaining of a wide spectrum, *perceptual safety net*—one that can catch us when and if our major weakness and fundamental inadequacy kicks in and could bring us down. We can become steady, focused, and aware drivers by understanding our anxieties at the wheel and how they relate to our driving behaviors. Even our acting out as drivers in ways we would never dare to exhibit in other social contexts becomes easier to understand. We also become better drivers when we understand that emotionality plays a huge role in how we all drive, whether it is because we are surrounded by a large number of unfamiliar people or simply because we are, in fact, *dealing with people when we drive*. Once we get a handle on the fact that driving is a super-charged social activity, we can better understand our urges and behaviors behind the wheel. They mimic how we behave or want to behave in other social settings. If we then add and give weight to the fact that we are "out of our neurological league", so to speak, in terms of crowds and the performance of precise highly consequential tasks, we can grasp the need to learn how to transform the way we drive and how we feel when we drive. With knowledge and awareness we can impose control on a process that otherwise terrifies us due to the unknown.

CHAPTER TWO: Review

1. Is driving a social or solitary activity? Explain.

2. If driving is a social activity, is it comfortable, fun, celebrative, and a place to meet new people? Explain.

3. Generally, how do we deal with other drivers in other cars?

4. Why is the social aspect of driving potentially dangerous for us at this point in our development?

5. How often have you competed, in whatever way, with a stranger on a highway, in a parking lot, or in city traffic?

6. Could you call other drivers or vehicles external distractions that have to be managed? Explain.

7. Why *might* women drivers be more aware of what is going on in other cars than are men? Speculate.

Notes

CHAPTER THREE
Focus, Awareness and Destination

If you have no idea where you are going, you'll take every detour and where you will end up, if you get there, is in trouble.

General D. Patreous, U.S. Armed Forces

One thing we have learned so far is that our brains are not sufficiently developed for the complex rigors of traffic. The part of our brain that handles what we do and with whom—that is, the social self—is repelled by the presence of so many others, by cars and people, and by the inescapable requirement that we proceed on course among them.[7] This, itself, is a major driving challenge, even though it has gone unrecognized and unaddressed.

---

7   To be precise, this part of our brain is a task-social point of orientation.

To cope with the arguable "insanity" of contemporary driving and our unsuitability for it, our brains and our psyches need a boost—in focus and more. In this chapter we will look, in more depth, at the key element of focus and the role that our destination plays in keeping us both focused and alert. We will also note why it has become more difficult for drivers to focus than a mere decade ago—particularly new, young drivers.

A Dual Focus Toward a Destination

Focused awareness, as briefly described at the beginning of the book, refers to our being focused on the road ahead and around us—and this, alone, is easier said than done. The element of awareness takes focus even further. It refers to the element that keeps us aware of and ready for the "predictably unpredictable". That is, we must always be aware of the fact that something could change, go wrong, happen to a driver ahead or beside us, that requires a defensive, instant compensation. This is how a professional NASCAR driver proceeds during a race. He is super-focused on his grip on the turns, his speed on the straightaways, and the tiny bumps on the route that could transform an accelerating, turning or braking movement into a lethal flip and smashed heap of cars. In addition, both the racing driver and the everyday driver have to remain aware of the human, competitive, personality and mood factors. All vehicles are driven by human beings with moods, problems, good or bad days, days with too little sleep and other factors that can affect a split-second judgment or reflex.[8]

------

8   All drivers should be mindful that an unexpected medical crisis, such as a heart attack, is one of the rarest causes of unfocused or erratic driving.

We are practicing focused awareness when we are alert to the possibilities that can arise as a result of a spontaneous mix of human actions and reactions.

However, as also indicated, *focused awareness is sustained simultaneously with conscious awareness.* This means that as we drive vigilantly with regards to everything that is happening around us (and regarding everything and anything that could happen), at the same time, we remain "conscious" of our own driving condition—that is, we are conscious of whether *we* have had too little sleep, have driven too long without a break, whether we are driving in a bad mood or in the midst of an emotional crisis and more. Conscious awareness refers more generally to an awareness of and focus on (and rectification of) our own state of mind so that we are not the driver who causes a serious problem on the road. Again, referencing the top racing professionals, they never go into a race without gauging their state of mind and managing themselves accordingly. They also learn what around them triggers or sets off certain reactions and behaviors so that they can reduce or eliminate the chance that something or someone will set them off, causing them to lose a degree of external focus. Top drivers know other drivers on the track, and they know what makes each other tick. As a result they can use tactical moves to gain advantage by either distracting a competitor or by exploiting a competitor's specific weakness or area of emotional-mental reactivity. As everyday drivers, we do not know our fellow drivers. However, what we can know is that first, we, as drivers, can make mistakes or take risks, and second, we can figure out and remain conscious of what makes us take risks as the result of certain emotions. These *inner distractions*, those that originate in our own emotional makeup, we can learn about and either limit or eliminate. Where other drivers are concerned, we can only remain focused and aware of the potential for driver "acting out". As we move further into this book, the reader will be able to see and discern various ways in which we all (some more than others) bring behaviors and reactivity to driving that underscore the need for focused awareness. Becoming aware of all this, combined with more thinking, discussion and conscious practice is how we become the "self-conscious", most focused and safest drivers on the road.

The link between our inner and outer focus is the ongoing awareness of, and continuous checking in on our *destination*. The fact that we should be aware and remain aware of where we are going seems somewhat obvious. It is easy to state with certainty that we never get in our cars to go "nowhere" or to drive in circles. However, if the reader thinks about it, there are odd exceptions. It *is* odd but not that rare that drivers forget where they are going and drive in an unplanned direction. All it takes is intense preoccupation or a distracting mental or emotional state to remove us from what we are doing. The element of destination, a sense of where we are going and why, is another way in which we remain focused and alert. Even (or especially) during a drive to a familiar, otherwise "memorized" destination. Regardless of the familiarity of our objective (destination), we don't drive the route the same way twice. As an analogy, if we are hours into the first part of a challenging, team climbing expedition, mutually dependent and unsure of an imminent change in the weather, no leader would throw the map aside and expect the team to make it to a base camp. On a climb, maps and the conditions of the route are checked and re-checked. The route is just as, if not more important, than the destination. It is similar, if not as "step-by-step" critical, with respect to driving. At this point, it is sufficient to say that having an ongoing sense of where we are headed makes us more attentive to our route and to what on our route might act as a distraction or obstacle even if the route itself is as familiar to us as our own backyard.

All of the above may seem self-evident, but the factors form a protective and "directing" focus that is notably absent from most drivers' approaches. They are distinctly absent when drivers get into the most common "wreckage producing" accidents. Without the triangulated approach to focus just described (focused awareness, conscious awareness and destination), we are bound to miss much in the way of warning, insight, and anticipation with respect to driver error.

The Techno Daze

Focus is critical and should be second nature to us, but it is not always easy. As we have learned, we have an innate, unconscious anxiety related to performing the task of driving with a "bunch" of strangers. However, there is another obstacle as well—and unlike the obstacle presented by our primitive brains, this obstacle has everything to do with how our developed brains function now.

To drive with extreme competence, we do need to focus on more than one aspect of driving a car. Without some kind of super, synthetic mind enhancer or refined psychic abilities, we are left with having to find a way to multi-focus in a way that we have never before applied to driving. Furthermore, the realization that we *need* to learn and to adopt a new kind and degree of focus in order to keep ourselves and others safe on the road comes at an inopportune time. It is ironic that just as studies are showing how everyone—regardless of age—concentrates and focuses less deeply and for shorter periods of time, we learn that it is urgent that we focus more, and differently, while involved in an activity common to virtually every adult in the developed world.[9]

We are at a historic point in our mental and social development at which our ability to focus is decreasing due, in large part, to our over-dependence on technology.[10] Innumerable studies exist that submit that the advances and prominence of technology over the last few decades, combined with the proliferation of "simplifying gadgetry" have changed the way we use our brains. In fact, it has literally limited our *inclination* and, therefore, our *ability* to persist in a state of acute mental focus. Not surprisingly, at the same time as we are suffering from what could be referred to as "lazy brain syndrome", the consumer market seems determined to limit us even further. Countless deflecting and so-called "helpful" and time-passing gadgets continue to come at us in a massive technological swell. We can (and do) purchase and affix to the dashboard and other corners of our vehicles sundry attention-grabbing devices meant

---

9   The need for a renewed focus is not just driving-related. We want a neurosurgeon to have led a life that honed her ability to focus and concentrate. However, the concern for a population's ability to focus, whether it is on reading, listening, or taking in data and nuances in other ways has long been and is a serious concern among scientists and pedagogues alike. See reference below.

10   Jaron Lanier, You Are Not a Gadget (New York, Alfred A. Knopf, 2010).

to make even a short drive less tedious.[11] In addition, at the same time, much about our lives, from the speedy, complex pace of a day in a working parent's life to push-button access to thousands of television channels (many of which can be watched concurrently), has left our brains agitated and, in effect, dulled or lazy. For passengers, long car trips used to be spent playing word or history games, geography and language conundrums, which hone both focus and memory. Now we have a million ways to deflect our attention without using our minds. Instead of trying to remember the date of the Magna Carta, we're watching *Rookies 3* on a flat screen—as a family in motion.

Re-learning to Focus

As drivers, we are lacking encouragement, enticement or any kind of enforcement to inspire us or force us to put more thought, attention, and focus into our driving. However, most adults and late adolescents do have something at stake that should provide sufficient incentive, even a fear of consequences that will make us *want* to adopt a new kind and degree of focus. The generally optimistic among us count on the fact that most people want to stay alive and whole, and to protect the lives and well-being of loved ones. Even the majority of drivers who

----

11 Indeed, a recent CNN report with the headline "Look, No Hands! The Driverless Future of Driving is Here" reports technology already in play can create autonomous cars that require only vehicle to vehicle communication to drive. That means we could stay engaged even more with our other gadgets. However, cars will still be dangerous since we are social animals even if our cars are not. We can override technology and blame it on the technology. Doug Gross, CNN, Feb 22, 2012. http://whatsnextblog.cnn.com/2012/02/22/the-sci-fi-future-of-driving-is-already-here

consider themselves "good-to-great" in the driver's seat, with nothing new to learn, can ponder the possibility that they can also, regularly, either save lives or keep others out of trouble. Whatever works to make increasingly crowded and inadequate highways and interstates less assuredly a place where, every ten minutes or less, someone will be hurt or killed.

The truth be known, each of us who has had over a decade of driving has unknowingly affected at least three other drivers in a deleterious or negative way. And not necessarily in a small or marginal way. Not all major accidents are the acts of the severely impaired or perpetually reckless. This is another powerful incentive to learn and practice as much as we can about the complexity of driving. Even when we are in the higher degrees of semi-focus, the odds can be stacked against our making a split-second correction so as not to add to *someone else's mistake*. The child who leaps out from between two parked cars to chase his baseball and is hit and killed instantly by a responsible, cautious driver, is both a prime example and the most frequent "helpless driver" accident on the books. Those who have seen, firsthand, the breadth and depth of grief, broken lives and families, even additional related deaths resulting from this particular type of mishap, find they have more than sufficient incentive to become the very best drivers possible. Consciously or not, this inspires an increased outward and inward focus and an ongoing, intermittent reminder of one's destination.

Driving Because We Can

In all fairness to most drivers (and as said often throughout this book), insufficient emphasis was put on focus or focused awareness when most of us learned to drive. The driving landscape has changed drastically over as little as a decade and there was much less known about the human brain and driving until very recently. Furthermore, the assumption that we all drive starting at a young age whether we are ready to or not, instills in us a false sense of confidence. This false confidence gives generation after generation of poor drivers permission to drive dangerously and generally unchecked.[12] However, there is another, cultural and social pressure brought to bear on parents and youth where driving is concerned. Driving as an "activity" is something in which we are expected to participate in ASAP. It is also something that would bring us some unpleasant social feedback were we to reject it for a time and simply *not* drive—this, at an age (for a new, youthful driver) when social heat can burn badly. The pervasive and persuasive message spread by the auto industry, aggrandized and sexualized in movies and on television, and further intensified in mere conversation in a consumer culture, is that if you don't drive and (God forbid!) don't own a car, you don't "belong". Thus the near panic to get our first car and the dubious generosity of solvent parents who provide an appropriate one for a teenage driver. This cultural imperative or expectation guarantees that every year untold numbers of new drivers are happily roaming highways and roads with too little skill, and worse.

In spite of the strain experienced by the majority of families that cannot afford to hand a teenager a car on his or her 16th birthday, there is nothing inherently wrong with doing so (under the right conditions) if parents can afford it and decide it is appropriate. Especially if parents impose the condition that the youthful, new driver *learns*

---

12 That is, until they have an accident.

to drive—that is, learns skills *beyond* those taught in the accredited and solid driving schools that teach according to ministry or state guidelines. First and foremost, the new driver must understand the life-saving necessity of driver focused awareness and conscious awareness, the optimal state of overlapping external and internal focus necessary for safety and efficiency in traffic. Then, the new driver can take it from there, learning more, and exceeding most other drivers on the road. As a bonus or by-product, the focused and learned driver commonly surpasses others in unrelated aspects of life precisely because of the kind of "thoughtfulness" and mindful, situational approaches sound drivers learn to apply.

Super-Focus

The two-pronged principle of *focused awareness* and *conscious awareness* is at the very foundation of responsible, safe and survivable driving. We are taught to keep our eyes on the road, but very few of us actually drive with our eyes closed. Most of us drive with our eyes vaguely road-centered, except for *dangerous* one to three second bouts of animated conversation, texting,[13] lost cell phone searches, lip-synching to a favorite song, determined body

---

13 As new laws were being proposed in Arizona to restrict the use of cell phones (for calls or texting) while driving, a study featured on CNN (Dec. 13, 2011) reported that a one to three second lapse in "on-road" concentration adds three car lengths or spaces to an otherwise immediate emergency stop.

scratching, even flirting.[14] These small activities, fidgeting and sundry other distractions, are potentially lethal. They are the *normal, common* mistakes drivers make and should stop making.

A better way to describe a solid driving focus would be to refer to it as keeping one's *mind* on the road. We cannot do much more than listen to a CD or half-converse with a passenger or with someone via Bluetooth (risky but legally acceptable) if we want to maintain a steady hand and mind. When we *fully focus*, we benefit by being able to remain aware of driver and driving dynamics, of our state of mind, of driving conditions at each point along our route, and of what is going on regarding vehicles ahead and around us. Even what most sensible people, good drivers and professional drivers consider to be a firm focus is too often insufficient. There is not a driver of any skill level who has not barreled at high speed along a super-highway and around a wide turn, only to find to his or her horror, that traffic, for as far as the eye can see, has stopped. The same driver jams on the brakes and perhaps tries to swerve to avoid the worst, half-hoping for the best but half-expecting, even waiting to CRASH! Even with what could be called reasonable focus, our brains do not compute that there can be hundreds or more cars, apparently, suddenly, "parked" on a highway, mere yards beyond what was a shared, high-speed set of concurrent lanes. This common situation does not require human error—depending on the speed at which one was driving. Traffic volume and movement can play

---

14   Flirting is not new to driving—and it is very common. This is yet another pressure on young (and older) drivers to drive a "cool" car. A cool car is almost as good a conversation opener as a baby in a stroller or a dog. Even when contact is made while in motion and in short spurts at lights or in traffic jams.

tricks on our sense of space, depth and speed. For some, it can also dull the brain, resulting in a kind of *reactive paralysis*. The only way to avoid all surprises and any blunting of our senses is to be ever-vigilant—to drive, regardless of traffic and other conditions, with uninterrupted focused awareness. When this becomes second nature to a driver of any age, he or she actually becomes a stabilizer, an element of neutrality or of safety positively affecting others in his or her proximity and beyond. This is guaranteed when a driver also takes on the responsible challenge of ensuring that she knows what makes her tick—both negatively and positively.

Focus and Calm

By necessity, to be focused, competent drivers, we have to remain conscious of the innumerable ways in which things can go wrong in the uneasy, high-velocity, competitive mix of traffic. However, in order to be able to do this, we also have to find our own way to create a base level of even-mindedness—basic mental relaxation—in and around our driver psyche. And we have to do this even before backing out of our parking space. Focused awareness and agitation are mutually exclusive. One cannot be upset or "wired" (as we tend to be) and aware at the same time. The driver who can get beneath personal and everyday tensions to a state of relaxed awareness is competent to drive. Otherwise, with low concentration spans, massive worries and insecurities, and an inability to get beyond our shared and individual turmoil, *many* of us should take "time off" from traffic.

Focused and Conscious Awareness as a Cause

It may sound simple. However, the author has already teamed up with a number of excellent drivers to make "responsible driving" a calling or cause. Good driving—teaching all drivers everything there is to know about fundamentally safe driving—is at least as important as teaching families that keep firearms in their homes about gun safety. People can inadvertently kill with guns—people also inadvertently kill with automobiles. You need a license for both, but the proliferation of both guns and cars throughout society has made it impossible to adequately control who uses them and how. Where driving is concerned, most new and seasoned drivers might be well-served by taking additional courses related to important, basic driving rules and traditional defensive driving skills, but there is a mental factor that is of greater importance. Even with the sound job done by driving schools that only have a driver for a handful of sessions, the schools do not have the information or the time to teach the necessity and nuances of the serious, overriding elements discussed in this chapter and book. Someone who scores 100% on a traditional written and practical driving test could still be a danger to herself and others. Rules and regulations, parallel parking, being able to point out blind spots and knowing how to use our vehicles' mirrors can be memorized, practiced and applied with a little effort. However, consistently competent and mindful driving requires more in the way of self-knowledge and awareness, including an awareness of the subjective unpredictability of other drivers.[15] A good, solid, mature driver also has to be someone who knows where she wants to go and is intent on arriving at her destination in a positive state of mind. Good, thinking people can make excellent drivers once they apply the facts, insights and tools in this book. Furthermore, many of us are convinced, the best, most socially responsible drivers are also our most positive and contributing citizens.

---

15 Subjective unpredictability is looked at further on in the book. It refers to the fact that each of us drives as individuals with a composite life experience, individual circumstances, and emotional and physical reflexes that vary and have different roots and causes. These variations alone are enough to make some super-sensitive, comprehending individuals virtually phobic about driving.

CHAPTER THREE: Review

1. Why is a life objective a "good thing"? How does it help us?

2. How does a life objective relate to driving and destination?

3. Why is driving alone in one's car a social activity?

4. How would you define focused awareness? Conscious awareness? Do they relate to each other? Overlap? Explain.

5. Why do you think a driver should not focus on the car ahead that is spinning out of control and off the road?

6. Think of a time when your mood affected your driving. Note whether you affected another driver, wanted to affect another driver, knew whether or not you affected another driver or just sang a medley of your favorite, musical hits.

7. Would you invite all drivers you pass or are near on an average drive to a party in your home? In or at a rented space? At the home of a relative? Why or why not?

8. Is having a destination when driving at dusk with few cars on the road less important than driving at mid-day in heavy traffic? Explain and discuss.

9. If someone is deliberately tailgating you (for more than six city blocks or five highway miles), how does it make you feel? What is the best thing you can do when this happens?

10. Are drivers who consistently change lanes to fill the space between one car and another focused? What, in your opinion, might they be doing?

11. How do the components of focused awareness, conscious awareness, and destination integrate to allow for safer and responsible driving?

Notes

Notes

CHAPTER FOUR
Two Angry Men—In Space and On the Road

Zoom... zoom...! does not define a journey and speed does not guarantee arrival.

Dr. Lauren, Lecture to Midland Secondary School District, 2010

Imagine the following stories of two family men, each of whom needed some time to himself and decided to go for a drive to get away from it all. Accept and enjoy the parts that are more than a little unusual.

Scenario One: The Astronaut

On the morning of a non-training day, a NASA astronaut became moderately frazzled by his two young children's squabble and his wife's efforts to cool them down. He had felt this way before and had a habit of quietly removing himself from the "crazies" by going to his workshop or for a run. This time, however, the brilliant scientist and space traveler felt the urge to take off, to just get away from the house and family for a while. And he knew where he was going. He grabbed his briefcase, got in his car, and headed to his beloved home away from home—the familiar confines of the space center.

Within a short time, the astronaut found himself at his desk. As he started to address some paperwork and review some technical data, it occurred to him to check out his locker, and fiddle with his flight suit and other items he would need for an upcoming shuttle. As he examined his suit, he shifted into a mindset where the peacefulness of space was palpable. His team was a well-oiled machine, focus was the name of the game, but existing in space itself was what the astronaut described as pure bliss. After a sigh and a look over his shoulder, he decided to use his official Commander passes to go further—just to check out his beloved spacecraft. Soon he was moving almost robotically toward the craft with all his gear.

The massive space jet was ready to go. He knew it would be. The shuttle had been more or less poised for launch for about a week. Except for the odd bit of tweaking here and there, and the normal, ongoing tests and re-tests of various systems, it was essentially space-worthy. The team had just been waiting for the imminent launch date and time. Our astronaut knew this. He also knew he could maneuver the ship with his eyes closed. Though he enjoyed the mutual dependence and division of labor shared with his team members, when he feasted his eyes and other senses on his craft, the team was the furthest thing from his mind. He was not thinking about the fact that each team member had to be able to take over the spacecraft in an emergency and get it out of trouble or down to earth via a safe, close-by sea-landing. In fact, except for his having started to habitually review procedures, he wasn't really thinking at all. He was already caught up in a mission. He was about to do what he loved most, alone and today. He was like a space cowboy, at high noon, defying rules and protocol.

He gave some explanation to a technician and got some help with his suit. Passing by and saluting a few more skeletal staff members on the entrance floor that leads to the spacecraft ramp and opening, he raised his helmeted head with pride. He had no sense of consequences—just pure excitement and anticipation about what he was about to do. By the time he reached the spacecraft, his muscles were tense, and he was alert, focused and emotionally as fine-tuned as a winning Olympiad. He settled into his seat, instructed support personnel to close the hatch, and began what everyone at the center that day assumed was an unscheduled instrumentation test and run-through, usually conducted by the full crew. However, by the time the countdown began, the astronaut had severed key computer links to the space center mainframe. He knew he would blast solo into the galaxy within seconds. Then, with no thought given to the shock and pandemonium below, he left planet earth. His destination? Precise coordinates—somewhere in the calm, perfect darkness of outer space.

Scenario Two: The Businessman and Driver

A hot-tempered husband and father was in the midst of an ugly verbal argument with his wife. They had always had a rocky relationship, but this time the husband took out his rage on ornaments and sundry breakables that he pitched at walls with bullet-like speed and precision. Barely aware of his actions, he did, however, sense his wife's fear and heard her tearfully announce the within-minutes arrival of their children from school. He grabbed his car keys and stomped out of the house.

The slamming door and cracking glass could be heard from a block away.

The man then screeched out of the driveway going way too fast, and backed onto the lawn across the street. He proceeded to swerve like a frantic fish, his efforts to get away digging into the spraying grass and dirt. As he revved the engine, the transmission straining under the acceleration, he neither thought about nor cared where he was going. He was just taking off! Driving! Wherever he ended up was irrelevant. He stayed vaguely within the part of the large city in which he lived, though he couldn't have been sure, speed-turning here and there, and then back again and then forward until, after almost two hours of random driving, he precipitously turned into the parking lot of a fast food restaurant and lurched to a stop. He sat, sweating, his heart still racing, his anger still evident to any who saw him. He didn't feel hungry. He didn't want to eat! He still wanted to drive, to just keep on going. To nowhere.

It was much later that night, six or seven hours later, when he drove into his driveway and cut the engine. He was pumped but exhausted, and a little disoriented. He couldn't have told you where he had been, where or if he had put gas in the car, missed stop signs or ran traffic lights. Now, he was back. It was time to go in and try to avoid facing the music.

Surveillance and the Two Angry Men

As unlikely as the first scenario is, somewhat like a poorly written "made-for-TV" movie, the second scenario is familiar to far too many drivers. The two hypothetical scenarios, allegories that start discussions about focus, destination and more, are used in seminar settings when teaching new and experienced drivers. Seminar participants are at once curious and amused—especially by the astronaut gone

AWOL with a chunk of complex, billion-dollar technology. Opinions are invited about whether the astronaut or the car driver has committed the more dangerous act. After tracking and discussing the moves and modes of transport that the two men resort to in order to "get away", participating groups come up with answers and explanations that spark more and more discussion. We usually start with the more familiar and identifiable case, the angry man in his car. Along with some interesting answers there is, of course, much identification—both with backing onto someone's lawn and, strangely, with the imagined, lulling effects of floating in space.

1. The Emotional Component

A. The Car Driver

The man driving his own car was enraged and heading nowhere until he somehow made his way home. The emotional component is highly significant. Needless to say, no one should ever drive when he or she is angry. Nor should we drive "unconsciously"—that is, without putting some thought into our mindset and driving both before and during the trip. No driving experience should be sporadic or unplanned. Clearly, if we "grab the keys and take off" we are not doing so with thoughtful intent. Furthermore, when we feel unsettled, restless, annoyed, disappointed or hurt, we are unable to focus in the ways described in the last chapter, let alone manage already overstimulated nerve endings. If we absolutely have to drive in a less than steady mood, we must adopt a heightened level of focus and awareness with respect to ourselves, to other drivers, and to traffic signs and signals. Experts who study driving patterns and who have determined that the majority of accidents take place close to home understand the role that heightened emotion plays in serious accidents. The term "close to home" means just that—a limited space or area in which we drive often and, therefore, in a wide variety of moods. Each of us can probably recall times we have found ourselves in our driveways, unaware of precisely how and when we arrived. When we drive the same routes repeatedly, we tend, dangerously, to drive with less focus and concentration. We can literally drive part of or our entire route in a rote repetitive mental state that can leave us with little or no memory of the experience. This mechanistic state allows us to further remove ourselves from the driving process by thinking, sometimes intensely, about something else. In addition, without what would usually be at least a basic level of driving focus, we are able to entertain wildly extreme emotions. Once our minds are off the road, there is no telling where they will go without responsible self-management. Getting into a car, especially in a familiar, much driven area, when we are already distressed is tantamount to having the intent to do damage. Our thinking, reactions and actions are seriously distorted when we are in an *anger*-induced state of arousal. Even our basic mechanistic skills sink to a level significantly below par. Anger also tends to attract anger, as well as to spread it. When we are in a state of rage, we are likely to be impatient and aggressive towards drivers with like emotions or, as many people are, at least ready and willing to fight.

Any extreme emotion, including extreme excitement, blurs a driver's focus. Unless there is a balancing factor, we should put off a planned errand or other short jaunt or trip until extreme emotional states have subsided. This, or learn, like professional drivers, pilots and others, to adopt a standard level of driver focus, one that predominates *regardless* of what else is going on in our hearts and minds. Needless to say, the driver in the allegory is not a mature adult and responsible driver. He was lucky—and so were others around him.

B. The Astronaut

In contrast, after years of unremitting training, jet or fighter pilots and astronauts enter a zone, a mental and emotional state of perfect balance before and during air and space travel. The balanced state of mind and the emotional "set point" that are habitual for astronauts include a neurophysiologic acuity of focus and function. The training and then the mental and physiologic experience of being in the cockpit neutralize all emotions other than those aligned with the thinking and focus required to handle what is essentially a massive, faster-than-the-speed-of-light computerized aircraft. The craft is designed to thrust upward and then perform maneuvers, and the individuals who take charge of it are also trained, in fact, indoctrinated, to manage the craft with consistent perfection. In addition to the training of the crew and the virtually automatic functioning of the extraordinary aircraft, the craft is also constructed, revised and adjusted to be *essentially* accident proof. The shuttle shuts down and will not launch if there is a mechanical problem that would put the hugely expensive space adventure at risk. Astronaut training and the design of the spacecraft neutralize potentially problematic factors, such as a rare case of astronaut restlessness. Once the astronaut is strapped in, he is acutely focused, calm and alert. Furthermore, the coordinates that mark the path of the spacecraft are preset and call for very little if anything in the way of steering, braking, accelerating, or keeping an eye out for oncoming traffic. There are, indeed, no stop signs or traffic lights. There are no intersections. Outer space is also bereft of the external problems caused by unthinking drivers.

In addition to the intense mental, scientific, cognitive and hands-on practical training required of astronauts, candidates for shuttle crews are chosen from among men and women who have already learned, and come to personify, emotional and mental self-discipline. Moreover, astronauts have been instilled with both persistent perfectionism and an unshakable sense of purpose, excellence and devotion to the mission—from launch to splashdown. As a result, shuttle problems have rarely if ever been due to human error, let alone due to human emotion.

The astronaut in our allegory did not take off under what we would call normal conditions. However, putting this aspect of the allegory aside, he nevertheless conducted himself in accordance with his training, another fundamental result of which is a pervasive loyalty to and mutual sense of responsibility among the crew. When an astronaut enters and positions himself in the cockpit, crew interdependence reinforces what is already a singular combination of focus, observational awareness, and responsiveness to the nth degree. Even without his or her crew, an astronaut is trained and disciplined to adopt a mental-emotional posture that guarantees objectivity, mutual respect, and collaboration.

C. The Emotional Winner

The astronaut is, without a doubt, in a more focused and balanced state of mind. The variables put in place by an angry driver, randomly meandering streets, highways and back roads, even in his home city, present a significant danger. The driver is not focused, not seriously inclined to protect those in the proximity of his vehicle (as the astronaut would be), nor has he had the kind of training that includes dealing efficiently with mild to major distractions. This includes, of course, not allowing oneself to be distracted by one's own emotional state. There has, clearly, been too little emphasis (and just a little lip service) given to ensuring that we drive with a cool head.

2. The Element of Destination

A. The Car Driver

Even though we look at the various elements of responsible, focused and safe driving separately in this book, they do, of course, overlap and are inter-related.

As we have learned, knowing where we are going at the outset of any drive provides a dimension of focus throughout the period during which we drive. Accidents happen more frequently when people either drive aimlessly without a solid destination or when they are in such a familiar area that they think less about every aspect of their driving, including their destination. As already established, the chances of a mishap increase considerably if, in addition to being unfocused, one drives in an extreme emotional state. Last minute turns, aimless steering, mistaking one-way streets or driving slowly in the fast lane or too fast in the slow lane usually happen when one is emotionally "off". Many of us have driven while deeply pensive and even this is dangerous. However, being both lost in thought *and* having no overriding sense of direction is a state made-to-measure for an accident. In the case of the driver in our story, both he *and* those who unknowingly came within a few cars of him that afternoon and night were in serious danger. As we will see, the context he created was significantly more risky than that created by our fictitious astronaut.

B. The Astronaut

In this admittedly unusual situation, the astronaut benefitted from coordinates built into and preset in the spacecraft's programming and hardware. In addition, the destination represented by the coordinates was familiar to the one-man crew. Even if he wanted to, the solo astronaut could not suddenly steer the craft to the lower skies over a favored Caribbean island or go beyond current parameters in an attempt to slam into Pluto. He would have early choices (and restrictions) and specific, to-a-tee return routes built into his not entirely adventurous joyride. Moreover, what this particular astronaut was after, we can assume, was the peaceful en route stage of actual space travel. So, in a sense he also had a destination, albeit one that was encoded in the technology. By the time the craft was set to return (and perhaps, in this story, set to do so at a time slightly adjusted by the astronaut), the captain would be relaxed, focused and, as was his objective, he would have, ironically, regained his comfortable state of off-duty relaxation. Regardless of what awaited the scientist and pilot when he splashed down, his ride was both successful and safe. We'll leave the story here and leave it up to our combined imaginations as to what the repercussions would be, in real life, for going on a joyride in a billion-dollar, government-owned spacecraft.

C. The Winner

Whether we are looking at emotionality, acuity of focus, destination, even conscious awareness, the astronaut wins hands-down over even the most experienced, nonprofessional driver. Furthermore, when and if an astronaut makes an adjustment in or toward outer space or when returning, there is no one else on the "road", other than the odd aircraft (taken care of by the computerized sensors) to consider. There are no double or single lines, no medians or other busy traffic factors. The social or interactive aspect, the primary source of danger in traffic, is absent.[16]

Another significant factor plays a role in these scenarios. The lone astronaut, unlike the miffed driver, was captaining in a state of optimal physical and mental fitness. This is mandatory for an astronaut who is part of a space program. The same could not be said for the driver. Regardless of how much the astronaut has to react to, he would have faster honed reflexes than the average driver. While overall fitness should be a requirement for wielding a fast-moving vehicle in a crowd, it is not. However, it is a fact that those of us who are fit are more emotionally resilient, more naturally focused and have faster reflexes, both mentally and physically, than the average individual and driver.

----

16 In spite of the hands-off, even "mind-off" technology that is imminent for new cars, none of the key "human" elements and requisites of driving can be eliminated. Driving will remain an intensely interactive, social exercise that requires understanding, keen attentiveness and several levels and kinds of awareness. Our humanity is "low tech" and will ultimately always play a factor in driving.

3. The Social Context

The Driver and the Astronaut—A Comparison

Driving a car, SUV, or truck is more than a matter of motion and direction. It is a complex task we perform not just in relation to rules and regulations, road conditions, and weather but also in relation to other cars manned by other people. All but the most insightful of solid driving instructors, whether they are professional teachers or harried parents, relatives, or friends, have left this critical element of modern driving unaddressed. In fact, the social or people-centered element of driving is, arguably, at the root of most driving close calls and deadly accidents. As drivers and mammals with territorial needs, we rarely drive in what can be experienced as neutral territory. We are almost always among other drivers and in danger due to driver unpredictability and the potential for spatial invasion, a factor that pushes our buttons about territoriality and our individual significance or viability. When we are forced to relinquish our space, it is usually messy and potentially injurious.

On the other hand, the space traveler virtually owns his space and does not have to worry about rear or side view mirrors. His landscape is sparsely populated. The absence of fellow travelers in space eliminates the most significant danger presented to drivers on the ground.

Don't Drive—Get a Space Ship

Clearly, were we able to drive our vehicles like astronauts or even pilots, we would be much safer. The forced intimacy among drivers puts everyone including passengers—in a two dozen or so vehicle radius—at risk. By driving, we make a decision to do the equivalent of skydiving with a novice group, all of us without instruction and without practicing how to open a parachute or keep it from tangling with others.

In the next chapter, we will look at another, more personal aspect of "social driving"—that is, driving with those close to or related to us. The more liberties we feel we can take with each other (and thus distract each other), the worse we are going to drive or behave as passengers. This is particularly true when it comes to driving with loved ones. As we will see, there is a delicate ego involved with respect to the assigned or self-designated driver. The word "driver" is a symbol of competent, respectable adulthood. Therefore, the impact of a passenger's reaction to or *criticism of* our driving has a distinct effect on our confidence, competence and pleasure at the wheel. Driving, though virtually an assumed part of growing up, has come to represent much that is vital to our sense of who we are, to our self-esteem and to our sense of significance in the adult world. In short, it is a sensitive subject, and can be a hotbed of conflict.

CHAPTER FOUR: Review

1. Why might an astronaut feel unnerved in heavy traffic? Explain.

2. Who, the driver or the astronaut, with equal driving abilities, would you prefer to drive with in a terrible storm? Explain why.

3. If you had to drag race with one, would you prefer to drag race with the driver or the astronaut/jet pilot? Why?

4. What do you think would be more dangerous—to drive a car while enjoying a sandwich and coffee or to be in space eating a hamburger and drinking a soft drink? Explain.

5. Which man—the astronaut or the driver—would be more likely to perform an illegal U-turn to return to get something he had forgotten? Explain.

6. How great a role did emotion play in indicating which of the two scenarios would be more dangerous? Explain.

7. Overall, who do you think went on a more dangerous jaunt? The astronaut or the car driver? Explain.

Notes

CHAPTER FIVE
Fatal Distractions

I can't drive with my mother. She's always yelping and grabbing the door handle. My father keeps telling me to signal sooner. I drive with them perhaps twice a year but even that is way too much! I'm a wreck after!

Steven P., 34 yr. old lawyer

In addition to the various cognitive, psychological, neurologic, and basic mechanical challenges related to driving, serious problems can arise when, as drivers, we take on individuals who are significantto us, those with whom we are intimately or romantically involved, spouses or relatives.

A passenger and driver in, for example, a new romantic relationship, drive in their own magical world and out of touch with much of what is going on around them. However, driving with a parent, a sibling or with someone we want to impress or to whom we need to prove something with

our driving prowess, can also be dangerously distracting. In short, we are profoundly distracted by passengers
with whom we have new, old or ongoing issues. In an ideal
world, none of us would ever be at the wheel of a car with
a passenger with whom we cannot be utterly ourselves.
Potent passenger distractions (PPD) can be as perilous as
a DUI.[17]

The Love Drug

New love, or the experience of falling in love, is literally a
brain-altering, biochemical experience. The shifts in our
biochemistry can result in weight loss or gain, giddiness,
preoccupation, memory interruptions, trance-like reveries
acting out (adult showing off), and various out-of-charac-
ter behaviors. Because the object of our love is always with
us, or on our minds and in our rapidly beating hearts, we
can be under the effects of new love—even when we are
driving alone. With or without our love interest sitting in
a car beside us, we function with much less of our rational,
linear, and logical brain. This means that all the rules, good
habits, usual reaction times, and other common aspects
of a good driver's driving are, unless we consciously make
them "kick in", partially suspended. It may be great to be in
love, but it isn't great to drive with a love-addled brain.

Driving, Love, and the Ego

We have ego needs related to driving. At the beginning of
romantic love, our egos are fed, even super- or over-fed
by the words or actions of a mutually "in love" partner.

---

17 PPD—potent passenger distraction? Why not?!

When this new and fuzzy stage of a relationship ends, even if it ends quietly, the new state may be, depending on a driver's maturity level, age and other circumstances, characterized by hurt, anger, humiliation, shame, embarrassment, sorrow, loss and more. The "end" and loss may be as extreme as the dreamy beginning. Our egos are fed but fragile in the good stages of new love, and bruised and fragile at the end. Falling in and out of love means that one day we feel as if we are King or Queen of the road and the next we feel like a chilled, lonely and shunned hitchhiker. By virtue of disturbing and confusing the ego (the psychic space in which lies our identity, sense of self-worth, and more), both the beginning and end stages of *being in love* interrupt basic cognitive rhythms. They also affect our behavior, dull our reflexes and, most importantly, drastically diminish our ability to *focus*. Neither state is conducive to basic or average driving competence. In fact, in the early stages of romantic love, in addition to being in a state resembling one that is drug-induced, we are trying on and playing various roles, versions of ourselves that fit better or worse with how we are perceived and received. Even if one role is that of the "amazing driver", we are role-playing, not attending to the various elements of driving. Our focus is our audience, not our destination, our surroundings, and the elements of our route or journey. In this misty love-fizzed stage, going for a drive means going off to be with each other in a state of unconditional, mutual bliss. Near the end of the relationship, going for a drive is equally as unrelated to intelligently managed movement in traffic. At both ends of the process of falling in and out of love, it is clear that the combination of driving and love bliss, or cars and crushes, is a volatile one. In that we are slightly or very "out of our minds", both states can lead, in short order, to some serious emotional crashes—but not as potentially deadly as the probability of a crash of a more literal kind. The powerful distraction of being in love, and driving with the object of these intense and at times baffling feelings, is arguably the most potentially fatal of the fatal distractions.

Back to Reality

With respect to traditional or nontraditional couples who have weathered a good number of years in a relationship, driving is recognized by mental health professionals and couples alike as a common source of friction. Related arguments are as common as those caused by finances or parenting, neglecting to put the top back on the toothpaste, or forgetting to take the garbage out. For most couples, the way in which one or both members handle a vehicle is a source of up and down, day-to-day conflict. Such conflict may be mild on a good day but intense on a day when other stressors have created a climate defined by raw nerves. In a culture where, in spite of economic hardship, owning two family cars is the norm, an estimated 40% of couples tacitly agree, after years of conflict, to drive separately. Even when there is an enduring love between two people, driving (and, often, what each partner wants as a showcasing, or merely practical, vehicle) persists as a significant talking point during arguments. It is also an area from which couples draw to insult or to push emotional buttons. Because how one drives is of both cultural significance (like body weight and looks) and significance regarding a couple's comfort and their family's safety, it is a loaded subject.

Second only to criticizing how a mate performs in the bedroom or is otherwise affectionate (just one ugly step before mocking a partner about his or her income-earning ability), couples deep in "car conflict" too often assume a degree of "car camouflage" and act out in vehicles in a way that neither member would be caught dead doing in any other social context. Furthermore, in a moving vehicle, distracted and dull-witted due to a loaded, blinding, and passionate argument, couples indulge in rough discourse (or worse) that puts them and others at great risk. Yet, we should by now understand why. Criticism or perceived criticism of one's driving by a life partner is tantamount to being criticized for being weak, unimportant, generally incompetent, and outside both the cool and normative cultural requisites for successful personhood. To be told that one is a lousy driver is, generally, a colossal put-down. In addition, each perceived or actual slight related to driving (personal viability) is stored away, making the most often designated driver (and often the driver by choice) both more sensitive to what might be criticism and more alert with respect to avoiding criticism. If couples decide to (try to) end driving conflicts, they usually find themselves reviewing related, if not as extreme, interaction in other aspects of their relationship. The alternative option, arrived at by some, is to drive separately, regardless of the destination—to work, on holiday, to visit a sick parent, to watch a child's baseball game, and any other activity. With gasoline prices ever on the rise, making the owning of (or for most people, making payments on) two cars increasingly difficult, this stress can exacerbate the very issue it was meant to resolve. Couples can benefit from discussing, with or without the presence of a neutral party, the roots and meaning or significance of habitual, driving criticism and related spats.[18] Any reasonable way of

18 It is useful to note that in North American culture, the male in a traditional relationship (and the member with the most power in other relationships) is, on the one hand, most likely to take the wheel and on the other, less likely to be criticized.

getting beyond what one couple interviewed for this book described as their regular and automatic "driving rages" is worth trying. Ideally, after doing some work in this area, two people sharing their lives can find a way to respectfully share the driving. Whether it is new love or seasoned love that is periodically distracting, what is needed is what has been emphasized throughout this book—some thought, (calm) discussion, mutual respect, and then focused and conscious awareness.[19] The agreed-upon driver has to, with support, launch into a managed emotional state as soon as he or she turns the key in the ignition. The potentially taunting passenger has to make a similar commitment. By making the choice as a couple, two people are also making a choice about how they communicate and about mending and preserving other aspects of their lives together.

Family and Friendly Ties

Driving with certain family members can be as irritating as a droning, predator deerfly in a pup tent. For adult drivers, older parents in particular can drive a visiting "adult-child" to a state of wilting distraction.

Even once we are on our own, families remain more complex constellations in our lives than most of us realize. Where driving is concerned, a parent's expressed (or otherwise exhibited) opinion of an adult-child's driving, even in the offspring's middle age, is beyond exasperating. One or both parents introduced most adolescents to driving and for a relatively extended period of time (for an adolescent)

---

19 Conscious awareness is integral to this process. If one feels he or she is going to "blow", pull over and get off the road. Couples have to work together at being conscious and aware of the build-up to, and imminence of, "in-car road rage".

most parents controlled the use of a vehicle. Furthermore, it is only as we mature that we see our parents' imperfections (as well as fine points), including those related to their driving. As an adult with one's own car, visiting anywhere from a semester to a couple of decades later, a parent's implied or open criticism of when and how their offspring brakes, how quickly one accelerates or how soon one signals, is met with a singularly thin skin. Even well after independence, there is an unconscious power struggle between child and parent. The parent takes on his or her old role as teacher and critic, and the adult-child comes with the urge to prove and maintain his or her autonomy and competence. In fact, there is no age at which the adult-child ceases to want the approval of his parents. Driving, the ultimate symbol of "maturity", legal independence, individual autonomy, even, in a way, of success, is an activity and process that is made-to-measure to disappoint. In the later, limited role of parent, this is one of the few areas in which a parent can feel as if he still has input and influence—even though it invariably backfires. In addition to both the role reversal and the adult-child's need for approval, the older parent may have become more set in her ways and more easily unnerved than a younger adult. If the driving style of the offspring is more assertive and agile than the parent's, that is, defined by a good measure of passing, managing speed limits, and launching competitively from stoplights, an unimpressed parent will likely show it. A parent who claims to be neutral but who grunts, gasps, braces himself with the dashboard, grips the door handle or makes "unconscious" motions to brake to ensure the driver takes note of his discomfort, is not going to win favor or extend a visit.

The extreme emotions evoked by parental complaints or expressions of discomfort do not all fall into the category of anger. Adult offspring come away from a visit the highlight of which would be the rough and regressing driving experience, with a genre of shame. Inevitably, the adult-child strains to show the parent that he is driving as a "grown-up". At the same time, the parent, unchanged, retro, and no longer relating in an appropriate way to his child, becomes infinitely more avoidable. In addition to anger, therefore, the adult offspring drives away with an added layer of sadness, fatalism with respect to pleasing his parents, and alienation. Driving represents a great deal about communication and interaction. It is also a metaphor for getting through life, taking responsibility and problem-solving. The mature adult does, at some point, come to a significant realization and it represents a kind of emotional rite of passage. Driving in a parent's neck of the woods, invariably brings the matter to the fore. Recognizing and experiencing the effects of the struggle for power, the adult driver realizes that there are some things that cannot be changed and, significantly, approvals that will never be won. For autonomous adults, the adage *"you can't go home again"*, translates into *"go home, visit, but expect the bedroom of your youth to look as if you never left"*, and expect a parent's reception to reflect the same.

Old Scores and New Scores

A somewhat similar tension often exists between younger and older siblings. Even in middle age, a younger sibling will want to prove that he has caught up (or even surpassed) an older sibling in skill and boldness, and the older sibling will want to hold his own. Regardless of whether the siblings are male or female, a life-long, post mid-adolescent competition can come down to proving one's skill at high speed, out-maneuvering the majority of drivers in a traffic jam or, another way to score points, showing up with a better, more expensive, high-end vehicle. Driving together, with one or the other as a passenger, presents the driver with a significant and loaded distraction, one that leaves no one focused on the road—and both driver and passenger in danger. As is the case with aging parents and our own maturity, someone has to "let go and let grow". One sibling has to opt out, as is the case with any duel, for the danger and the competition to pass and recede into the past.

We can all find someone with whom we would be delighted to settle a score. If we have access to someone from our long-ago past or bump into such a person as part of our and his adult life, we might even remember why we feel the need to prove our strength, our need for respect, or our right to recognition. Wanting to settle an old score is natural—however, we have to reach a level of maturity (by say, age 25 to 30 if we are lucky) when we realize the feelings and related issues are not worth the torment. Needing to pursue the illusion of evening things up from another "lifetime", says something about our ongoing need to gain respect as a driver *and in our lives*. It is a sign that we have maintained old, personal and private psychological needs and open wounds that cause distraction in ways well beyond driving. If we ever feel uncomfortable, not ourselves, or if we are unusually pumped about driving with someone, we should stop and ask ourselves why. Each of us can figure out whether or not we can be mindful and maintain or restore self-conscious awareness and focused awareness *before* we get behind the wheel. If we cannot, we have no right to the car keys.

Loaded or intense relationships affect our thinking, our moods, and our judgment. We can be with people whose presence or company agitates us or aggrandizes us. Either way, by so doing, we are inviting a distraction into our driving process. We can choose to suspend good judgment and drive in a state of temporary biochemical bliss. Or we can take on a passenger to whom we want to teach a lesson. Each "high meaning" connection we have with a "special" passenger changes the driving process into something else, usually something from another time and place, and a potentially fatal distraction.

In the next two chapters, we will look at a variety of driving or task styles that encompass most drivers and many of us in whole or in part. They speak graphically to the fact that we have to be aware of how we are driving, in different moods and, importantly, how we drive in relation to how we perform and behave in other areas of our lives. Just as importantly, we have to learn what we are up against in the way of the styles and inclinations of other drivers. Part of being focused and aware is knowing what to look for, what we are seeing when we see it, and what to do to remain disengaged and as safe as possible.

CHAPTER FIVE: Review

1. Explain in your own words the meaning of the statement: *"Beware with whom you drive"*.

2. Explain *outside road rage* and *inside road rage*. How might they be related?

3. Why do you think couples fight over how one or both members drive? Explain.

4. Is it okay to own a car and be in love? Explain.

5. Have you ever been a "bad" passenger? Describe the situation.

6. Why, in your opinion, have in-car, interactive factors related to life-saving or dangerous driving typically not been discussed in courses, schools or by teaching parents?

7. Have you ever competed with a friend while and by the way you drive?

8. Do you think you would like the "focused driver" as a person? Explain why or why not.

9. Why do well-trained dogs make great passengers?

Notes

Notes

CHAPTER SIX
Unpredictable Strangers

All he does is find fault. He's always looking around corners for the next crisis. As a result, he's always swerving and has caused three accidents.

Elizabeth, about her ex-husband

There are as many variations in driving "types" as there are personalities. In addition, there are as many driving oddities as there are moods and emotional ups and downs. All of us co-exist with a variety of responsible and irresponsible people, as well as caring and uncaring folk whom we would or would *not* want to have any influence over our lives or the lives of our loved ones. The adage, "you are the company you keep", speaks volumes about each of us and our lives. We have choices and we instinctively, and with reason, grow closer to some and keep our distance from others. However, this is not the case when it comes to the social environment in which we routinely risk our lives.

While driving, we share small sections of pavement and presume a common adherence to single and double lines with strangers of all kinds, all with their own agendas, personalities, and passing moods. The only control we have, which is often too little, is to remain acutely and consciously aware of our driving environments—both inside and outside of our vehicles—and to drive with focused awareness and an appropriate sense of responsibility. This includes understanding, as best we can, and in general, what kinds of drivers are on the road with us.

As we will see in the pages to come, normal (let alone extreme) people approach tasks and activities, including the act of driving, in vastly different ways. Each of us drives among others with what are frequently completely different ways of perceiving what we are doing and how it should be done. Furthermore, what offends one driver, does not offend another. Some drivers look for offenses or problems while others drive carefree and are rarely upset by other drivers, road conditions, or the odd bout of extreme weather. There are extremely angry drivers who are easily set off and who can trigger their own anger, and there are furtive or sneaky drivers who get a kick out of appearing out of nowhere and startling a driver into a hazardous swerve. An actual "true crime", there are even drivers who deliberately set out to use their vehicles as weapons.

My Way or the Highway!

It is the fact that drivers generally wield a vehicle in such a way so as to protect themselves and their cars, with a further limiting *driver subjectivity*, that is the cause of most accidents. Virtually all new and experienced drivers, confident, comfortable, entitled (to safety) and spared the lifeless realm of statistics, do, in fact, drive as if they are closed off, separated from, and destined to be untouched by other cars and drivers. This posture has perpetuated a deadly illusion and represents a mindset that is the opposite of what is required for driving that is smart, safe, and much less dependent on sheer luck.

I Do It My Way!

Subjective driving further illuminates the fact that both young and more experienced drivers are hard-pressed to view themselves as doing anything wrong or that inconveniences or puts others in danger. We all drive in ways that reflect how we address other aspects of our lives and approach other activities, whether they are work, recreational or family-related. We have habitual ways of doing and performing among others that, in other social environments, are not always as unfettered or, frankly, as easily tolerated. For example, if the task and communication style of a manager in a major corporation results in low profits and a demoralized employee population, he or she is severely sanctioned. In virtually all work and social contexts other than driving, there is a bottom line, a cut-off point of acceptability. Unless a driver's approach or subjective task style causes a number of *serious* accidents (in relation to which, for example, he or she could ultimately be charged with a criminal offense), he or she can pretty well wreak life-threatening havoc at the turn of a key. Even if insurance premiums do rise per accident, longtime habits, especially unchallenged ways of doing things, still die hard. We can, as drivers, get so mired in our styles and usual ways of operating that, unless we are forced to look at ourselves in relation to others, we assume we are doing just fine—and, more important to the average ego, that *our* way is the right and only way. This tenacity of habit, our long-held approaches, and our individual subjective sense of *how driving is done* is what can—and does—drive others into the perennial ditch.

Subjective Driving and Chance Encounters

A critical aspect of this book is understanding that there are complex, individual driving styles in a social context in which there is no room for error. First, we have to come to grips with the fact that we are people driving and interacting among and with people, and second, we have to consider the fact that individual personalities, quirks, moods, disturbances and habitual ways of performing play a fundamental role in our shared driving experience. Our habits and ways of approaching the task of driving affect others. Conversely, the task styles and driving habits of each and every driver on our new and familiar routes affect us. As if the stakes were not sufficiently high, drivers also bring individual ways of reacting to the gamble. We all self-distract and react according to how, in the first instance, we go about the driving process.[20] Aggressive drivers, for example, usually react with aggressive defensiveness. In the second instance, we each bring—to each reactive and head-on experience—all the factors that determine who and how we are and act, in a significant moment, on a spe-

---

20 Imagine four strangers mowing an arbitrary 12 acre section of lawn—with different mowers, different ways of mowing (some in rows, some in circles, some in small squares), under varying time constraints, of varying ages, levels of intelligence, experience, tempers, moods, ethics, and pride of workmanship. The work would grind to a halt due to chaos or conflict—or more likely, both.

cific day, in our separate lives. Just think of the odds of a smooth, uneventful drive home from work.

Profiles in Driving Styles—Recognizing and Responding to "Difference"

To learn, absorb and then to bring an understanding of driving styles to the road, read and think about the five styles presented in this section, and answer the questions at the end of the chapter. Then proceed to the following chapter and do the same with the second set of styles and questions. Continue to imagine and think about the styles, think of people you have driven with, and see if a particular style of driving comes to mind in relation to them. Be sure to note styles that resonate with your own approach. There will be an almost immediate shift in your driving perspective and applicable knowledge. That is, you will, very soon after learning about driving styles, become a much less subjective and insular driver.

Driver Speak

Each style is preceded by a direct quote from a driver representing the style. What people say when they are under duress (and even when they are not) says a great deal about how they drive and perform other tasks in their daily lives. Words and behaviors are yet, additional, easily accessible hints that can help us decide whether or not to jump into the car of a colleague or associate offering us what seems like a convenient ride home. Just as importantly, if we start to *listen* to our *own* utterances, they can take us "behind the scenes" of our own bad, if long unnoticed and/or accepted habits. This latter focus can give us a revealing sense of just how much we have been dependent on luck to keep us safe, and how much on focus and skill.

PROFILES I

1. THE CATASTROPHIZER

Damn, look at the $%##!! traffic! It was just fine before you made us stop! See?! SEE?! Damn YOU! And damn every idiot on this damn highway!

Starting with one of the most dramatic yet common ways of approaching processes and tasks, the catastrophizer is someone for whom anything not planned or anticipated represents the end of the world. A car taking too long to pass or a slight slowing of traffic is sufficient reason for the catastrophizer to go into a mental, usually very verbal meltdown. This driver is easily and seriously distracted, quick to anger and loses focus over the smallest occurrence. Needless to say, driving with this kind of person is extremely unpleasant and unnerving.[21] One doesn't, for example, dare touch the radio, adjust one's seat or open a window without asking permission. Even *asking* for a change in the car environment (for example, per the preceding, asking to turn on the radio) can induce irritation or the classic, catastrophizer rant. However, even without a passenger, the driver will find something to rail about and someone to rail at. When he is angry or upset (which is often) a catastrophizer commonly pounds the steering wheel with the ball of his hand, gestures madly and spits

---

21 The catastrophizer has a very hard time repressing his tendency to rail against everything that he deems stupid or irresponsible. He has little respect for others, and no patience.

profanities and phrases such as "*I KNEW it!*" when there is any kind of small wrinkle in his plans. Furthermore, the catastrophizer's reaction to someone (or to a vehicle) that might have caused what he perceives as an inconvenience is usually ugly and often retaliatory. He is likely to react to a perceived offense by, for example, catching up to a passing car, driving alongside it, and gesticulating madly, spewing threats and reprimands at the baffled and nervous occupants. Alternatively, he might overtake the offending vehicle (or, better, cut it off), get in the lane in front and hit the brakes, leaving it up to the other driver to avoid a rear-end collision.

Without going into the innumerable examples of how this driving style rears its usually ugly, style-distracted head, it is sufficient to say that even on a good day, having to stop at and wait for one red light can ruin this driver's (and his passenger's) time on the road and beyond.

As is the case with all task styles, the catastrophizer's driving style reflects how he performs in his life off the road. If he were barbecuing with family and friends and a burger slipped to the ground, he would most likely stomp his feet and the meat, call his audience names, and leave the scene in a huff.[22] He then further de-focuses in a state of active rage. This self-perceived "good guy" (among "bad and lesser guys") is always on the verge of self-distraction due to his need for the impossible—a completely smooth ride and life without common wrinkles and even small surprises.

---

22 The catastrophizer is usually male due solely to the fact that this kind of behavior—from childhood on—would not be as readily tolerated in a female. With the same inclination, a woman would have had to learn another way to process her super-reactivity.

How to Recognize the Catastrophizer

Although there are short periods of time when a catastrophizer coasts along like everyone else, the following list of attributes can help to identify the style.

1. On long drives, the catastrophizer does not like to, and usually will not, stop at rest stops—either for himself or for a passenger. If he has been forced to do so, after rushing everyone through the process, he is clearly annoyed and further rushes his passengers back into the vehicle.

2. After passing a vehicle, this driver looks back, via the rear view mirror, in anger for being forced to break his driving rhythm and pass.

3. Unprovoked, catastrophizers are steady, serious drivers, whose vehicles swerve little and are kept at or near the speed limit.

4. He is often seen dramatically gesticulating at someone in his own car.

5. He or she typically drives a steady, solid, neutral colored, mid-sized car. Nothing fancy—too much can go wrong.

6. He leaves more distance than necessary between his car and the car in front of him—double to triple the recommended chevrons. When the space is soon filled by another vehicle, he is distracted (furious) and might tailgate the intruder until he feels he has made his point.

2. THE CAUTIOUS DRIVER

Don't talk to me! I have to concentrate! See, there's a car you can already see coming up behind me! Now, shhhh!

The truism that overly cautious drivers can be almost or just as dangerous as reckless drivers is accurate. This driver has taken caution to an extreme and then turned it on its head. Real caution implies care for oneself and others while performing a task. However, the cautious driver, who is a fearful driver, maneuvers self-protectively and with no regard for other cars or their drivers.

One form of "super caution" typical of this driver is a commitment to low speed (or no speed), regardless of the situation. This includes positioning herself in the fast lane on a multi-lane interstate, 30 mph under the speed limit. The fast lane will only be relinquished when the cautious driver senses (belatedly) that she might be safer in another lane. Under extreme pressure and unable to think clearly or quickly, she might choose the exit lane in which to drive and to lie low but with no intention of exiting.

The cautious driver is also the unfazed driver of the extremely slow-moving, leading car of a forced parade of over-heating, bumper-to-bumper vehicles on a two-lane highway. He is unmoved by honking cars veering in and out to check for possible passing opportunities, and by the even more dramatic and dangerous last resort taken by drivers who dare to pass, heading into oncoming traffic.

Unpredictable, the cautious driver's movements or apparent decisions are fear-induced, not rational or reasonable. By driving this way, the cautious driver remains fearful and successfully shuts out all data or activity on which most drivers make common, strategic decisions. He is among the drivers most out of touch with the social, interactive and spatial aspects of driving.

Perhaps needless to say, the cautious, fearful, self-protecting driver does not risk using rear or side view mirrors. He keeps his eyes forward, focused on the slow-moving pavement before him. Instead of wanting to, needing to or risking checking on what others around him are doing, he drives as slowly as possible in order to be left alone, safe, and unfettered by other vehicles.

This driver has only a vague sense of destination—with checkpoints often missed, thus demanding back-tracking and odd maneuvers. She is bereft of self-consciousness or self-awareness and would argue until she is blue in the face and white-knuckled (from gripping the wheel sufficiently hard to practically make imprints) that she, unlike other drivers, is merely *a safe and careful driver*. In fact, however, her lack of attention regarding what is going on around her regularly creates highway havoc.

The cautious driver is one of every driver's worst nightmares. However, as the reader will see, some drivers, depending on their style, will react to (be distracted by) the cautious driver more than others. Styles clash.

How to Recognize the Cautious Driver

1. Cautious drivers drive slowly, take significantly more than the average amount of time at a stop sign, and enter highway exit ramps at near "zero" speed.

2. She gets visibly agitated when a transport truck turns into her lane and drives in front of her. She

will not pass but rather will decrease her speed or even leave the road until traffic clears.

3. This driver typically sits upright, leaning forward into the well-gripped steering wheel.

4. The cautious driver appears to be concentrating intensely, as if driving through a blinding snow or rain storm with TNT in the trunk.

5. The cautious driver does not feel the need nor does she want to risk moving her eyes or head to check rear or side view mirrors.

6. He is often seen swerving in surprise and fear when a vehicle approaches unnoticed and passes on whatever side and in whatever lane has been left available.

The cardinal rule is to stay away from these drivers. If one does get caught or trapped in relation to him or her, it is best to relax, focus on one's destination and avoid further distraction. This driver style commonly provokes drivers to take risks, whether by passing under dangerous conditions, moving into an inside lane, or even flirting with using the median.

3. THE OPTIMIST

I could just drive and drive and drive. I just love it. I mean, movement and swaying along the highway with the wind coming in the window, what's not to LOVE?!

The optimist is a happy-go-lucky driver whose frame of reference does not include possible mishaps, accidents or the vagaries of other drivers. She or he uses the basic mechanical devices on a vehicle for steering and speeding up and slowing down but does not view driving as requiring much more. This is a naively confident driver who feels (and states with certainty) that driving is second nature to him—that he could drive any vehicle across the country without stopping to eat or sleep, and in an uninterrupted state of competent bliss.

Driving *is* perceived as a "no brainer". The female version of this driver might casually apply polish to her fingernails or toenails while at the wheel, and more than a few admit to doing their makeup while steering with their knees. Furthermore, this is the driver whose car is most often seen barreling down a hill without anyone appearing to be at the wheel. The optimist is merely searching for something that has dropped to the floor, confident that she has ample control or time to regain control should something come up—such as a cliff or an oncoming truck.

It is important to give this driver a very wide berth. The optimist is, more often than not, unconcerned about what is going on around her. She has no sense of the fact that human unpredictability lies at the core of and defines traffic (and life), and that, even when one appears to have the road to oneself, focusing on the surroundings is critical to accident prevention.

The odd behaviors exhibited by optimist drivers are epitomized in how they deal with the commonly conflict-inducing matter of parking. One could say that, "*the optimist always gets her space*". If an optimist driver sees an empty or soon-to-be-available space from afar, she or he wastes no time getting to it. While most drivers look for others who are already honing in on the same space, optimists do not. They do not think to do so. In fact, once they reach the space, there could be four cars vying for the one spot and optimists will just swing into the space and prepare to disembark, carefree as a kitten playing with a ball of string.

How to Recognize the Optimist

1. This driver frequently swerves and recovers.

2. The style is such that the driver, alone or with a passenger, appears fidgety or busy—because she often is.

3. A bumper might be hanging off this driver's vehicle or the tires might appear to need air (or replacement). The optimist does not remember to service or note the condition of his vehicle.

4. The optimist does not speed up for but regularly drives through yellow-turning-red lights, utterly unaware of the danger inherent in doing so.

5. The male optimist shaves at the wheel. Both male and female optimists typically flip mirrors around while driving to attend to their hair or for some other non-driving related reason.

6. This driver is known as someone who, if she is driving to an appointment or social gathering, will be late. With no planning, unexpected problems and distractions arise.

4. THE NEGATIVIZER

Every time I drive this highway it's a mess! And every time the same morons are taking up space! Then there's the damn construction! All these as-h-l-s standing around talking!

As a manager, parent, driver or even a shopper, this person is not "happy" unless he is noting and reacting negatively to something. As a driver, this posture and approach starts the minute he gets behind the wheel. It may be a regular complaint about and struggle with fastening his seat belt or the feeling that the tilt has been changed on his steering wheel, but unless he is profoundly and unusually preoccupied, he will immediately find things to complain about.

In traffic, the mere presence of other cars is irritating. Though this is an unconscious, spatial issue for all drivers, for the negativizer it is both conscious and consistently distracting. In the rare instance when there is nothing overwhelmingly obvious to complain about, the negativizer can go on about the ugly color of a particular model of car, the fading of the white lines that demarcate driving lanes, the presence of an abandoned broken down car at the side of the highway and so on. However, when it comes to vehicles that are in his proximity, moving, turning, braking and accelerating, the negativity can be off the scale.

Another style that is hard on passengers, this driver complains when he is overtaken by another car, regardless of how he is passed. He either verbalizes directly or indirectly to his passenger, thinks aloud or otherwise dialogues about the passing car going too slowly, too fast, swerving or otherwise playing games. A vehicle behind him is either tailgating or hanging too far back, planning some kind of offense. Stoplights are too long and there should be penalties that include jail time for the "creeps" who acceler-ate through amber lights. In that this driver can find fault everywhere and anywhere, he is perpetually distracted.

If the negativizer is or feels offended, at his worst, he can be retaliatory. In spite of the fact that he is generally not a speeder and drives quite conservatively, he is known to chase and tailgate the offending vehicle and hurl insults and profanities at it or its driver throughout the chase. In the same retaliatory mode, this driver is likely to pass, then slow down beside an offending vehicle and offer a generous array of hand and finger gestures, and mouth obscenities that can be lip-read from a mile away.

This is a profoundly distracted driver. He doesn't need anyone to fight with, but he appears to be caught up in a constant battle against things he deems to be wrong. He is the epitome of a driver in a very bad mood. His task style is most prevalent when driving, precisely because his attitude and unconstrained expressions of negativity are unacceptable in other social settings. Regardless, whether he or she is driving with passengers or otherwise engaged with others, this person, restrained or not, is not alighting to others.[23]

How to Recognize the Negativizer

1. At his best this driver is steady—driving within the speed limit, signaling turns and lane changes, and generally adhering to the rules of the road.

----

23 As is the case with the catastrophizer, overt negativizers are pre-dominantly male. A young, middle-aged or older female could not consistently exhibit and express negativity and be viable in social or workplace environments.

2. He can be seen ranting and gesticulating when stopped for a red light or in slow or unmoving traffic. One should not assume he is talking, hands free, on a cell phone.

3. If he (or she) catches a passenger looking at him in the above or other situations, he might retaliate in kind but with mocked exaggeration.

4. He drives a very old, apparently cherished vehicle or a high-end car. Both provide much room for potential problems, expense, and worries.

5. This driver can often be seen leaning away from the wheel to listen for imagined car problems.

6. In all seriousness, this driver, if accompanied by passengers, drives with people who look as if they are being kidnapped. Passengers are typically quiet, still and low in their seats.

7. The negativizer can tailgate, cut off another vehicle or perform side-by-side intimidation with what appears, from some distance, to be a steady skill-fulness. This distinguishes him from more reckless types of drivers.

8. This driver is among the most vocally or otherwise openly displeased over the loss of a parking spot competition. Horn blasting is common.

5. THE SIGHTSEER

I have my own touring vehicle—my car! I can take a friend, if I want, and just enjoy the sights. I know them all—their history, what's going on, everything! I could actually give tours! But I love to drive and discover new places more.

Like other drivers, the sightseer is, for the most part, more distracted by her approach to driving, than she is by other vehicles, road conditions, car problems or the weather. Regardless of where and why she is driving—to get groceries, on a road trip with a friend, to take her dog to the vet— she notices and usually commits to a running commentary on everything. Her commitment and focus are locked into her interest in colorful billboards, new housing construction, sunsets, cloud shapes, landscapes, license plates, people, animals, trees, and anything else that catches her eye and interest. In an urban or dense suburban area, she will notice people and describe how they look, how they dress, whether they look happy or sad, are laughing and more. With some of the characteristics of the optimist, this driver can have half a dozen near misses in a ten-mile drive and have noticed nothing. While she does mean to obey traffic signs, she regularly goes through stoplights and fails to notice stop signs. She drives with little interest in and with virtually no focus on driving. She would deem the concept of focused awareness an utter bore, as "much ado about nothing" with respect to her delight in the simplicity of sightseeing. For this driver, the maneuvering of her vehicle in traffic is the least interesting and compelling aspect of being on the road. In fact, if she were forced to pay attention to other cars and to adopt a basic level of driver focus, it would be the end of driving as she enjoys it.

The sightseer drives as if she is a passenger. Her eyes pan across the road periodically but, more often than not, she is fixated on something outside her car and beyond traffic. In addition, as part of what is almost a fidgety form of driver's attention deficit disorder (DADD), the sightseer, whether alone or with a passenger, further distracts herself by narrating incessantly.

As a driver who can enjoy a piece of architecture and talk about it even as she is, for example, parallel parking, she is a danger on the road. The basics of driving come easily to her and she is positive and not prone to anger or aggression, but she is both a distracted and disinterested driver. She is also incredibly lucky. Though scrapes and fender benders are not uncommon, it is a miracle that these drivers are still around to sightsee into their senior years. Others around them might not have fared as well.

The sightseer can run a red light while she waxes poetic about a sunset, and while four other cars and their drivers spin out of control. If this driver is in a small accident, the sightseer experiences the incident as a minor inconvenience, one around which one does all the right things with police, exchanging insurance information, exhibiting courtesy and concern, and tying up all the administrative loose ends. The only consequence that matters is whether or not the sightseer's vehicle is fit to drive. If it is, she is good to go. She proceeds without blinking.

A remarkable study in good fortune, unless and until the "tour" ends badly, the sightseer's driving reflects the way she lives. She is someone who is likely to have never had a specific objective or plan for her life and, not entirely unhealthy, she claims to live life to see where it takes her. She or he can be accomplished in a career or a hobby but this, too, is fortuitous. She is usually involved in an income-related activity that she likes and that allows both time and mental space for sundry unrelated interests. The sightseer does not worry about changes in her workplace, downsizing or job loss. Her keen and enthusiastic observations in all life environments (except traffic!) keep her balanced and, apparently, happy. Without any lessons learned, and no matter how deep or hot the water is or gets, these folk *seem* to float.

Like all things too good to be true, these drivers are no doubt tied to serious accidents involving obvious driver error. They are too often ignoring of traffic to beat the odds. As harmless as they perceive themselves to be, as drivers they are extremely dangerous. Missing an interstate exit and blithely reversing just off the pavement to get back to it, crossing four lanes in a last minute decision to park and hike a nature trail, or regularly, and with good humor, barreling the wrong way down one-way streets can only go on for so long without serious consequences.

The only way this driver style and mindset can be jerked into reality is through friends and family. It is common that people come to refuse to drive with the sightseer. This is not, by far, a "deal breaker"—the sightseer enjoys his own company and narratives but he also enjoys sharing his discoveries and insights. Significant people or a life partner might be able to broker a deal that involves driving lessons, new rules, and guarded company for one short drive at a time.

How to Recognize the Sightseer

1. The sightseer exhibits a great deal of head movement as she or he pans the landscape for interesting visuals.

2. The sightseer swerves mildly when she is "in control" of a vehicle and to an extreme degree when she is consciously, mildly correcting her course. Others see the sightseer as an erratic driver.

3. This driver is unusually animated, especially with hand gestures and nodding and tilting of the head.

4. The car that forces another vehicle off the road and into a ditch, but keeps going, is not necessarily willfully leaving the scene of an accident. The sightseer might not know she has been involved.

5. Sightseers commonly leave a turn signal on for hundreds of miles—or until they stop for or run out of gas.

6. This driver is disinterested in the condition or servicing of his or her vehicle.

7. The sightseer is inclined to drive a compact-to-sporty mid-size car of whatever color is available at the time of purchase. She likes the feeling of being able to handle a car without having to pay too much attention to it—but it must be sufficiently spunky to quickly and efficiently get him or her out of trouble.

CHAPTER SIX: Review

1. Think of two people you know and have driven with who inadvertently (in whatever way) annoy people on streets or highways or both with their driving.

2. As a new or seasoned driver, would you say you have been, until now, a focused driver? Explain.

3. Think of a driver (or person) whom you would describe as a potential catastrophizer. What would a long drive be like as a passenger with a catastrophizer?

4. Would you want to work for a negativizer? Explain.

5. As a driver and as a person, what is the difference between a catastrophizer and a negativizer?

6. How do you think the sightseer would function as an employee in a position in which attention to detail is critical?

7. How can you predict what a cautious driver will do?

8. What is the difference between the optimist and the sightseer?

9. Is it possible that people with any of the styles described in this chapter actually enjoy driving in itself? Explain.

10. List and try to think of a phrase to describe each of the five styles that were introduced in this chapter. (Go back over the styles if necessary.)

Notes

Notes

CHAPTER SEVEN
Even More Unpredictable Strangers

Sometimes I don't even want to drive any more! I swear the roads are full of nutcases.

Terry M.

In the last chapter, the reader was introduced to the concept and the reality of our bringing communication and task styles to the roads and highways. We learned that both how we are inclined to interact and how we perform tasks are reflected in the way we drive. If one has never before viewed driving as a social and task-oriented endeavor, the catastrophizer, cautious driver, optimist, negativizer and sightseer can come across like comical characters in a driver's nightmare. They seem too "far out" and too dangerous to be true. If only that were the case.

In this chapter, we continue to look at some major task and driving styles. By the end of this chapter, the styles will be well on their way to becoming part of your conscious and unconscious driving mindset. As you probably already realize, understanding driving styles assists us to better understand other drivers, to be less reactive to their actions, and to more accurately predict their next move. They also give us a way to address our own driving habits and "oddities" - and we *do* have them.

PROFILES II

1. THE E-RACER

If they don't like it they can get off the &*$#! road! If I knew who complained, I'd....

Most of us who have been driving for a while have learned to keep our eyes, ears and other senses open for the e-racer. However, regardless of a reasonable level of vigilance they still seem to appear out of nowhere.

The e-racer—the wild, usually young, super-speeder who drives as if he is playing a "crushing and crashing" video game prefers to *perform* on highways where he can better use speed to his advantage. And he often works in twos or threes. The e-racer weaves through traffic and super-accelerates (and then brakes) to prove his prowess. He is long gone if he has caused an accident and "e-rased" vehicles, if not people from the road.

In spite of how effective he or she is at terrifying drivers or causing serious accidents or messy near-misses, this person-driver does not feel as if he is part of the traffic community. This is part of his problem. He has bought into the fast and furious car culture but has little status in it. He usually has the same challenge in his day-to-day life, so he continues to seek an alternative status as a "road warrior". His style is, in its way, punitive. He may be going somewhere, but his driving kicks come from his perception that he is dominating and frightening other drivers. He commonly drives a small, older, customized car with dark-tinted windows, and usually works on his car himself. He or she is conflict-driven and fatalistic but self-aggrandizing in his verbal and other communication. He is a patent outsider and loner. He lives the way he drives—without purpose, and acting out in short bursts of destruction, usually by preying on others. He does not waste time considering either a future or the consequences of his actions.

When this driver is caught after a tragic accident, he typically says, "*I was just fooling around*". He is a weak, camouflaged, highway bully who turns cowardly when he has to face the official music.

How to Recognize the E-racer

1. This driver usually drives alone, without a passenger.

2. He or she (usually he) most frequently drives an older, re-vamped vehicle.

3. He is, in or out of a vehicle, isolated and insular by choice. Super-tinted windows are the norm.

4. This driver sits low in the driver's seat, head tilted downward with his eyes raised and forward-looking. He wields a covered steering wheel with one hand and is partial to wheel knobs.

5. This person has virtually no face-to-face exchange with other drivers.

6. He is often driving with a suspended license and battered or indistinguishable license plates.

2. THE PERSONALIZER

I swear every time I drive anywhere, traffic lights always turn red letting other cars through but not me, the same ignorant creeps tailgate and then cut me off, a psycho tries to run me off the road, and, if I have a passenger, she's mad at me. If I didn't have to drive, I'd stay away from all of them. It's pure punishment as soon as I leave my driveway.

Imagine perceiving everything that happens around you as a personal attack, whether it is road conditions, the weather or the actions and movements of other cars and drivers. Most of us, for example, find being honked at in what is evident anger to be both upsetting and personal. However, if we are personalizers, we experience honking as an even greater, more vicious and personal assault. With everything *feeling* personal, this driver brings layers of habitual defensiveness, as well as a ready martyrdom to traffic, and he adds new layers virtually every time he or she drives. For example, the mere proximity of other vehicles is a threatening distraction, raising the personalizer's expectation of an advertent or inadvertent assault on him and his vehicle. A fearful, "mal-focused driver", the personalizer is his own worst distraction and enemy.

This nerve-wracked person's approach to just about everything and everyone is to expect and therefore, more often than not, to induce an apparent or real affront. By early adulthood, the personalizer has developed an extremely defensive posture. The commonplace scenario of competing for a parking space best shows how the personalizer perceives himself on the road or generally in relation to others. If, for example, the personalizer waits with some frustration for a spot, he takes personally the fact that the "parker" is not moving with sufficient speed to vacate the spot. Then, he virtually loses emotional control when another vehicle slips in before him. Invariably, the personalizer will have words or worse with the "spot-stealing" driver. Depending on the task style and approach of the driver who edged in ahead, there could be a parking lot showdown.

After each common traffic challenge, each perceived as a direct or indirect slight, the self-endangered personalizer becomes angrier and more defensive. Furthermore, the longer he drives, the more inclined he is to retaliate or to attack before being attacked himself, just to make sure he gets his licks in.

Passengers thinking of riding with a personalizer should think seriously about taking a bus or cab. The personalizer interprets everything a passenger says and does—a shift of position, a sigh or yawn, even a pre-sneeze gasp, let alone a suggestion that an alternate route might be better for avoiding heavy traffic—as being personal and critical. Regardless of gender, personalizers are entangled in silent or overt battles in almost every moment of their lives.

How to Recognize the Personalizer

1. The personalizer looks skittish. He will steal a quick glance into the passenger window of a passing car as if studying who is within and what might happen to him in relation to the vehicle.

2. Personalizers usually stay in the middle lane on a highway. They anticipate being criticized or hassled for passing or for how they are passing. They worry about inciting criticism or an incident.

3. When they retaliate, they do so severely and with as much anonymity as possible. They usually drive alone. *If* they have a passenger, there is commonly no interaction. In the rare instance of communication with a passenger, it is accompanied by the kind of stiff, quick-movement gesticulating that comes with distress.

4. The combination of slow, defensive driving, and the checking out of other drivers, indicates a lack of focus on where they are going and why. They keep their eyes open for trouble, not for progress.

5. They drive non-controversial, medium to older model cars of plain colors or, at the other pole, high-end muscle cars as a way to project strength, confidence and belonging.

3. THE LEADER

I don't waste my energy judging. My job is to get me, or my passengers and me, somewhere safely and as pleasantly as possible. It's up to me whether I get involved in other people's crazy driving and I choose not to.

This rare driver is an asset on our roads and highways. He or she has taken what she has observed over many years and what was modeled for her as a child, and combines natural skills and wisdom with formal learning. She enters the driving world a good driver and continues to get better due to a keen interest and an understanding of the privilege and its related responsibilities. Add intelligence, insight, good reflexes and an acute sense of the dangers inherent in driving and one has a driver who can genuinely enjoy driving and make it safer and more pleasant for others. She is consistent in her actions and interactions on the road and off, thereby creating safe and respected spaces when among others.

In a quiet non-deliberate way, this driver attracts a following in her various life environments. Able to distance herself emotionally from the competitive herd, she is actually a *safe* driver to follow. Due to the fact that she is not focused on the car in front of her and drawn to follow in its tracks, she is also the safest bet as a fellow driver amid difficult weather or other challenging conditions.

Further and logically, this individual raises children to be good drivers without having to explain or say a great deal. If children are exposed to solid, smart and mindful driving, they will emulate what they know when it is their turn to join the world of traffic.[24]

As a rule, the leader drives neither too slowly nor too fast. He knows when to use speed to get out of trouble and has no qualms about slowing down to stay away from the fray of blatant competition and other dangerous situations. He also has no compunction about pulling over and off the road completely in the name of safety.

None of the above characteristics make the leader a serious or solemn driver. In fact, his confidence and skill allow him to, as stated above, enjoy driving—a mindset that is also

---

24 The exception to the rule is the child who gets lost in other ways as well.

passed on to those for whom he is a model and mentor. Furthermore, his enjoyment of driving actually makes him more innovative, creative and sharp. Just as the musician who loves to play his instrument reaches new levels of skilled expression, the relaxed and competent driver does the same. On a more practical level, the "rules" related to driving come naturally to the leader. For example, he or she is naturally committed to the visibility triangle—to automatically checking the rear and side view mirrors—requiring very little head movement to assess his position among other cars.

This driver performs the activity or process of driving with the least number of inner distractions. As a self-aware driver, he has figured out (in life and on the road) that holding on to old, problem-creating habits and bringing them to work, driving, or to other social situations is destructive, self-impeding and does not present a path forward that is satisfying and successful. Whatever imperfections this person and driver has, they do not show up in an interruptive way as he processes life or when he moves respectfully along the pitfall-ridden path of traffic.

How to Recognize the Leader

1. This driver starts and stops smoothly, neither racing to get ahead nor staying back from the bulk of vehicles on the road. There are no unnecessary, non-emergency jerky movements.

2. An observing passenger will notice a check of all mirrors, as well as speed, at regular intervals, with very little head movement. His eyes are rarely off the road.

3. This driver will react/respond to problems with other vehicles before most other drivers. Even (or because he is) in a relaxed state, he is focused and aware at all times. He is able to anticipate what another driver is doing or might do and to ensure his and others' safety.

4. While other drivers are reacting to an accident, construction, or some other inconvenience, this driver is trying to figure out the best thing to do, whether there is a need to call 911 or just move on and out of the way.

5. The leader does not interact negatively (or positively) with other drivers. His driving style is to facilitate movement, not to teach or reprimand.

6. This driver looks comfortable in the driver's seat and checks mirror angles, seat position and other comfort and safety factors each time he gets into a car.

7. Leaders are equally distributed between men and women—but their competence and confidence are rooted in and evolve for different reasons.

This quality of driving comes with learning more than the basics and then maintaining a keen interest in the nuances of driving and traffic. However, the consistently excellent driver is also thoughtful, responsible and confident in his or her abilities. Furthermore, though not naïve, this person trusts life.

4. THE ENFORCER

It may not be my job, but idiots who mess with me pay! It's what I DO!

We have all seen them—and, under duress, some of us have been tempted to take on the role and the behavior. The enforcer is like the unofficial rule stickler in the workplace, the pedestrian who scolds a stranger for crossing the street before the "WALK" sign, or the driver who leans on her horn when a driver ahead is a split second late in responding to a red light, turned green. She or he is prone to dole out punishment where she deems punishment is due. However, the vast majority of the time, the mishap or action that catches her attention is either not worth it, none of her business, or something of which the so-called culprit driver is unaware.

As annoying as they can (also) be to their passengers, enforcers can be dangerous when they are doing their self-assigned "duty". The enforcer is basically an adult bully. It is not uncommon for the enforcer to follow or chase down a car when he feels slighted by misbehavior affecting him or others. He is more vigilant about whether or not other drivers are "behaving" by his standards than he is with respect to his own driving. And enforcement means punishment, a non-verbal reprimand in the way of tailgating, cutting off offending drivers, alternately hitting the brakes and accelerating to confuse and unnerve a driver and, a standard and often concurrent action, performing the perennial "horn assault". Regarding the latter action, enforcers are horn fiends. "Horning" is a successful way of rattling or taking out a driver they deem to have made an error or to have been disrespectful. While many drivers may not know exactly where their horn is (but should know, in order to use it defensively), if he could, the trigger-happy enforcer would wear his in a holster—always loaded and always ready to intimidate.

Enforcers can provoke their targets into a kind of duel. We have all seen mad maneuvers—a dangerous dance between two cars, one of which is often trying to opt out—that force other vehicles to react and to try to avoid collisions. For the targeted driver, the key is to do everything in his or her emotional power to suppress the inclination to fight back or to react at all. This is no small order. Our instincts are to self-protect in the already uneasy gathering of too many people separated by and in moving objects.

There is no doubt that in taking on this bizarre role, the enforcer brings personal beefs and inclinations to our roads and highways that he exerts in other environments. Just as one would give this person ample space in a work environment, usually the best way to deal with this danger-ous driver is to stay in position or to back off and out of his way. Somewhat like a shark circling shallow waters, if this "policing" driver does not get a ready dose of enforcement, he will move on and "officiate" elsewhere.

How to Recognize the Enforcer

1. This driver is vigilant and usually in a state of spe-cific or non-specific anxiety. He overreacts to small movements and trivial changes in traffic patterns.

2. The enforcer positions himself snugly in the driv-er's seat, commonly keeps his hands in a tight grip on the steering wheel and slowly but noticeably peruses a limited driving and driver landscape (up

to six cars ahead and one to two lanes on either side) for driver misbehavior.

3. Small courtesies are absent. He is self-distracted by looking for an opportunity to mete out punishment.

4. If one is stopped beside a vehicle driven by an enforcer, one would notice that both the enforcer and his passengers appear to be silent. He wields the same kind of "corrective" power with his passenger(s) as he does with other drivers.

5. A sudden, seemingly inexplicable acceleration and lunge into different, sometimes ever-changing lanes is common practice.

6. For social, psychological and other reasons, the enforcer is more likely to be male than female.

5. THE VICTIM

My wife says I'm paranoid but I know when I am cut off deliberately or forced to drive too fast to be safe. Drivers get at me 'cause I drive sensibly.

As is the case with many driving or driver styles, it is a discomfiting experience to be a passenger with a victim driver. However, though other driver styles directly and indirectly affect passengers, the victim needs to share his narrative and *have it confirmed* by those who are with him. In general, victims are compelled to verbalize and to seek confirmation and empathy for the fact that they are being forever worn down by "terrible, cruel drivers" who are out to get them.

Someone with a victim mentality lives a constant melo-drama centered on himself. He can find a perceived slight even on an empty back road. When he is in traffic, it takes very little (if anything) for the victim driver to distract himself over how unfairly or brutally he believes he is being treated, threatened, left behind, forced to drive in ways against his will, and whatever else can be interpreted as happening or conjured by his imagination. For example, the victim will react and take personally something as small as the car ahead making it through a green light when he did not. It is as if all situations are created so that he will lose and others will win. With this perspective, he drives anticipating and watching out for the next slight. The victim shares some traits with the personalizer but is dif-ferent in some fundamental ways. While the personalizer takes everything personally and is inclined to retaliate for being singled out, the victim does not go after his perceived attacker. He prefers to be overwhelmed or overpowered by his victimization rather than take pre-emptive action. It is more the fact of being victimized (and the accumulation of incidents or proof) that "satisfies" the victim driver's narrative. A passing car that splashes water on the victim's windshield is deemed to have dealt yet another blow. A parking ticket is a woeful experience quickly shared, even by phone if necessary, as yet another indication of the fact that life and driving have had their way with him.

This driver was most likely bullied in school and likely holds an unchallenging job or position that he dares not question. As such, however, he deems himself victimized by co-workers, management, or customers. In short, he sees himself as, and indeed becomes, the center circle on the dartboard of life.

The victim driver presents a serious problem in traffic because he or she is not focused on driving. On the contrary, he is focused on or constantly awaiting the next victimization. Alert to be hurt, he misses much that is going on around him. When he *should* react objectively to a dangerous moment in traffic, he cannot do so in a safe, timely manner.

How to Recognize the Victim Driver

1. The victim driver looks around while he is driving. He is on the lookout for the next dirty trick or attack.

2. With or without a passenger this driver talks or "shares" a great deal while driving.

3. These drivers can suddenly take on a jerky or erratic driving style as they recover from a perceived slight.

4. Victims are commonly late at signaling lane changes, at noting and acting on detour signs, even at noting that a police officer has driven up behind them. This is due to their preoccupation with the next victimization.

5. The victim driver is just as often male as female.

As is the case with the other types or task styles, the victim's *style is her distraction*. Though this is the case for all driving styles, the victim adds another layer of detachment from his driving by his need to share, to describe and make the case for his victimization. And she will do this whether someone is present or not. The victim presents what is arguably the clearest case for the theory that an individual receives and reinforces what she thinks about and fears most. The victim is, in fact, her most formidable foe.

Primitive Fear, Styles and Traffic

Our task or driving styles help us to cope with *and* deflect our full attention to or from the intricacies of dealing with other cars, high and varying speeds, changing driving circumstances, driver idiosyncrasies, and much more. Traffic is, in essence, an intense social setting in which our ways of processing or our task styles "kick in" and then are exaggerated under a specific and untenable mix of psychic and physiologic stress. Given the essential, if inadequate role that our task styles and related coping mechanisms play, they cannot be changed overnight. On the other hand, however, the consequences of not increasing our awareness of (and ultimately managing) our driving styles over our basic work styles, are related to life and limb, not mere criticism and slow advancement.

Remember that our task styles alone ultimately fail us in traffic due to our primitive fear of functioning among "too much and too many", a sensory and psychological combination that is unfamiliar and threatening, and for which we are not, as humans, sufficiently developed. The overnight advent of motorized vehicles and then, just as suddenly, of traffic, have thrown us together in a process in which we perceive ourselves as separate but in which we are intimately and inextricably linked. Hypothetically, like a dangerously warped version of the primitive hunt, we are a hundred unfamiliar hunters (instead of three to five friends or relatives) all scrounging in a small space, with unknown, individual weapons, and without a shared objective other than survival. This is a classic, historic atmosphere for human fear, defense and attack.

It is in this post-modern state of unfamiliarity and unpredictability, the "unnatural" state of traffic, that our fundamental ways of doing things become defensive, at best, and offensive at worst. Without a conscious and concerted effort to impose reason over habit we perform or drive with deflected focus and diminished capacity. This is the fundamental reason that more people of all ages are hurt or killed in car accidents in a year (in North America and elsewhere where "everyone drives") than in all other forms of transportation combined. For an activity that has become a questionable, massively expensive national pastime and the presumed, entitled, first choice for "around the corner" travel, we are lousy participants.

Awareness is the key to change and change in our accepted, traditional approach to driving may come on the cusp of a revolution in car manufacturing. Smaller (and *smaller*), lighter, but no less speedy vehicles give the average driver and her passengers less protection against errors in judgment and an absence of unfettered focus. It's time we learned to drive, and we can start by learning just how perilously unaware we have been about the process. And, how lucky.

CHAPTER SEVEN: Review

1. Of the driving styles discussed in this and the last chapter, which best describes you, if any?

2. Is there anyone you would prefer not to drive with? Who is this person and why do you not enjoy driving with him or her?

3. What do you bring to the driving experience that is a little or significantly quirky?

4. Who is the best driver you have experienced? Why?

5. Name the driving styles described in this chapter. If an "undeserving" driver were added, how might his driving style have been described?

6. If an "entitled" driver were discussed, how might she drive and with what attitude?

7. Compare the styles of the victim driver and the leader.

8. Have you ever acted as an enforcer?

Notes

Notes

CHAPTER EIGHT
Gory Stories and Brain Freeze

I worry about my wife and kids driving. I talk and talk until they just roll their eyes and leave the room. Crazy driving is worse than ever. It's as if people are in some kind of panic, as if they're all trying to outrun each other. Driving today is just insane!

State Trooper, Mass.

This chapter has been controversial. More than a few people with years of marketing "smarts" were adamant that this section be in keeping with television and movie goers' attraction to shock and awe—full of gruesome photos of accidents, capturing the moments when people's lives went from "normal" to "over". The author has, however, held firm in her conviction not to resort to such photos, which would amount to nothing more than the gratuitous exhibition (and exploitation) of the victims and their still-grieving loved ones.

Learning theory has already established that we do *not* learn from negative images and that, in fact, they have a numbing effect on the reader and viewer. Already inured to horror by our appetite for reality TV and the 24/7 streaming of global news, we do not need further anesthetizing against tragedy and human suffering, especially when it results from our own ignorance and accepted incompetence. If those who slow down and risk lives to get a good look at the victims and carnage resulting from a major accident continue to do so, this is their choice, and their poor judgment.

Social Shockwaves and Extreme Driving

The subject that best serves the reader near the end of this book is one that *re*-presents and emphasizes the current *community* context in which we are driving. Increasingly, accident reports and police renditions indicate we are driving under a new and potent psychic strain, one that social scientists say relates to changes in our lives, in social and economic structures, and with respect to our expectations and sense of security. The majority of the North American population, primarily a middle-aged demographic group but also young adults who are trying to kick start careers, are carrying the extra mental weight associated with the fear of receiving pink slips or not finding a suitable job in the first place. There is also a related, pervasive fear of the future. As a result, *distress* and other anxiety-related emotions are closer to the surface and render us all less adept at managing our impulses and reactive behavior. At the very least, we are less likely to think before acting, especially when trapped among strangers, bumper to bumper, between thin lines, at high speed.

We Drive as We Live

It really hit in 2008, but it is a new and ongoing reality. Still amid the psychic shift experienced by the North American population in the aftermath of 9/11, personal and family financial challenges have people both frightened and feeling helpless. In addition, significant national and global events, influences, and trends have put a media-manic world and population on a mutually and contagiously distrusting edge. In addition to feeling a general sense of chaos and a whopping insecurity about the future, the majority of the (especially North American) population is coping with some degree of fear, and no small amount of anger over what has changed and been lost. Network and other media polls, as well as social scientific studies show that we are feeling less hopeful, more frightened, and more likely to distrust and find fault with others than we are to trust and engage. For the first time in the lifetime of most, a significant proportion of the population is unnerved and desperate for new parameters from within which to manage their lives. Intense emotions lie just beneath our social surface or at a level of mind where we are less likely to be able to decipher threats and manage defensive-offensive mindsets and actions. This has and does not bode well for how we function in the already messy, unruly community that is post-modern traffic.

Human Need and Brain Freeze

Our most primitive needs—to feel safe, secure, fed and in control of our life environments and our communities— create the foundation for our stability, sanity, and ability to function. When these basic tenets of our lives and fundamentals to our mental health are undermined, we feel uncertain about our present and future security and, as a result, we are generally reactive and more prone to "fight or flight".[25] The distinctly unthinking among us—the constant catastrophizers, personalizers, negativizers, those with victim mentalities and others—are in high emotional gear. Given this overall mood or posture, we have to be careful. We have to be almost *super*-conscious of our behaviors in environments in which there are only loose guidelines, a lack of fundamental civility, and too few enforcers of the law. Clearly, this pertains most distinctly to driving. None of us can risk behaving at the wheel of a vehicle in a way we would not dare to behave in an important social or business environment. However, studies indicate that we are not doing too well. We are behaving more cautiously in school, in our businesses or work environments, but many more of us are acting out more often in quasi-anonymous settings such as large grocery stores or in unavoidable line-ups. Many more of us consciously and unconsciously take out our frustrations and fears, and express our anger, when we are let loose among each other in traffic.

Social Emotions

This brings us back to the most significant aspect of this book—that is, we drive, in good and difficult times, *among others*, in a community of people in small- or medium-sized aluminum, steel and plastic units on wheels. We bring fear, anxiety, grief, or suppressed grief (anger) to a mix overflowing with human social and mechanical incompetence.

....

25 "Fight or flight" is a primitive biochemical, physiologic and psychological state into which humans shift when they feel threatened. See the classic book by Herbert Benson and Miriam Klipper, The Relaxation Response, HarperCollins, New York, 1975.

Anxieties, worries and the anger often associated with "change we don't believe in" further stunt our thinking and blunt our reflexes. This in turn evokes more anxiety and further dulls our thinking and limits our abilities. One insecure, angry and fearful driver affects everyone else on the road. Currently, as dim as this sounds, the driving environment can be compared to a crowded and frenzied city in low-vision darkness, in which we are all anonymous and armed. This is a dramatic image, but it is reflective of the collective mindset, of the shared *social* conditions on our roads and highways.

Being Socially Conscious

There has never been a more important time to learn to be a "social driver". Remember, that until now, the vast majority of drivers, including those reading this book, will not have thought of driving in a socially conscious way. Nor have we merely forgotten lessons taught recently or long ago, or skimmed over in a driving course. It is the opinion of mental health professionals and others that none of us has been (or is) taught a sufficient amount about interaction, connection, and interpersonal behavior as they are best applied in *any social setting*. This particularly pertains to the driving environment. We see poor behavior—road rudeness, fights with drivers swerving and cutting-off other drivers, angry honking, and worse—but, encased in vehicles, we have been unable to make real connections. We have also been permitted to avoid looking into the eyes of the reality that well-meaning but risky, thoughtless or aggressive behaviors in any kind of traffic can change or ruin a few dozen lives in a mere instant.

Best Visuals

If these pages could benefit from visuals, the author would choose shots of intelligent, responsive moves made by either learned or professional drivers. Were it possible, there would be well-done videos of how best to pass a slightly swerving, nervous driver, how to respond to a clearly aggressive cut-off, how to fall back safely in a crowded, dangerous traffic field, and more. Seeing these would be instructive and also might introduce the element of heroism into driving. The images might inspire better, more conscious driving. As is the hope for this book, a few clear images might prompt a significant "re-think" about how, why, when, and under what conditions we visit each other between the lines.

Currently, *we* are the scared and scary strangers among us. It is our egos that flare or deflate in the rough play of traffic. Moreover, it is our fear and insecurity that, without thinking, will compel us to have to prove our place in the fast lane.

CHAPTER EIGHT: Review

1. Generally, why is driving a "full-brainer"?

2. Would you want everyone to drive like you? Why? Why not?

3. Do you see yourself as generally reactive or responsive at this point in your life? How about when driving?

4. In your opinion, are racism, sexism and other "isms" expressed more often by a person while driving or while engaged in other activities such as, for example, having her or his hair profession-ally blow-dried?

5. Is "checking in" on our driving a big thing?

6. How often have you met someone in traffic whom you want to date?

7. Does it upset you when someone behind you honks when a light turns green? Why or why not?

8. You have received what you think is an unjust ticket and, after a half hour, the police drive off. How would you drive, when they and all other traffic patrol men and women, are long gone? Explain.

Notes

Notes

CONCLUSION
Follow the Yellow Brick Road

As long as you stick to guiding principles and focus on your destination, you will manage the challenges and climb to the mountain's peak.

Allen Proctor, *Everest Team*

In *The Wizard of Oz,* Dorothy was wise to do what was repeatedly suggested by those who wished her well. She was told to keep her destination in mind—Oz—and to follow the yellow brick road to the one place from which she could be sent back to Kansas. However, as clear as the path to her destination was, there were many distractions along the way. She could have detoured at any time. She could have been too frightened by the Lion and turned back, too closed to open up to the Tin Man, and not sufficiently focused to sense the sad warmth of the Scarecrow. Even the Wicked Witch did not, in the end, distract her from her goal.

The metaphors aside, the story of Dorothy and her journey has all the ingredients of *focused awareness* (and conscious awareness) as described in this book. When she was confronted with a number of scary and confusing distractions, she remained consciously aware of where she wanted and needed to go, of her surroundings, of those around her and of herself in relation to them. In spite of the chaos and calamities, she remained focused, mindful and alert. This is both the magic and the essential message of *The Wizard of Oz*—particularly as it relates to our adventures in this book.

The Real World

The good news for those of us driving in the "just as crazy" real world is that by merely reading and thinking about the concepts and facts in this book, our attitudes toward driving will undergo a shift. Readers of this manuscript have already reported that they are driving in a more conscious and insightful manner.[26] It is yet to be determined how long this change of approach and perspective will last without some conscious effort, but so far, those of us concerned with introducing a new approach to driving are optimistic. Even with the advent and hungry acquisition of hyper-deflecting gadgets and other "in car" technologies— "must haves" in almost every family car—the principles and information in this book should leave the reader in good stead for a positive shift in his or her approach to driving.

....

26 As part of ongoing qualitative research on driver behavior, a pilot study was performed in which drivers were asked to read this manuscript and drive normally for two weeks. Self-reported behavioral changes included leaving more space between vehicles, and a reduction in aggressive behaviors.

Choice and Change

It is possible, even with social and cultural factors affecting our focus, steadiness of mind, and our fiscal priorities, to revise the way we teach driving to new drivers. It is also, as the author and others have already seen, possible for those both more experienced at the wheel of a vehicle and more aware of their mortality to change old driving habits. In particular, it would appear that addressing the confounding social element of driving in a conscious and explanatory way has a transforming, positive effect on both the new and seasoned driver's psyche. There is also significant evidence that further introducing and equipping drivers with parameters for focus—including the focus on destination, on external and internal distractions, and on the role played by driver mindset or perspective—allow for a more conscious and managed driving experience. Human beings work more efficiently, rationally, and effectively when they have a sense of (increased) control and *response-ability*. Knowledge is not just power, it is empowering. The fear and reactivity associated with the "drive by the seat of your pants" approach that has long been the norm is substantially reduced when we have a fuller understanding of both what we are doing and how better to do it. Drivers benefit almost immediately from eliminating the essential denial about what this high-velocity human activity actually entails. For most, this will be sufficient to usher in a new respect for and approach to this otherwise potentially deadly, distinctly social process.

We are not androids or automatons and we can drive better and feel better driving when we merely make the choice to keep certain principles at the fore of our thinking. We can know that, as a result, when we drive we are less likely to maim or to be the victims of the same. This alone, on both a conscious and unconscious level, lessens the unspoken strain of performing an otherwise unnatural task that, whether we have known it or not, has been anxiety-inducing and, to a degree, stupefying. Along with more efficient vehicles and the increasing urgency of the uphill challenge for better ways to fuel them, we can choose a concurrent course of responsible efficiency. We can pave a course with parameters that enable us to change the way driving is approached and stem the flow of statistics that show we have been driving blind, and too often way off track.

With an earnest desire to undo old habits, apply new knowledge, live consciously and focus, we can have our own homing version of the yellow brick road.

CONCLUSION: Review

1. What are the major differences between being a driver in rush hour on a highway and being a member of a platoon patrolling a potentially enemy-populated ridge? Think of degrees of control.

2. Why would anyone say that when we drive on a crowded freeway, we are alone?

3. Why is a *response* better than a *reaction?*

4. Might someone be a better driver just because he or she has had military training? Discuss.

5. Explain what the expression "You are how you drive" means?

6. Will you as a driver and the way you drive change after reading this book? If so, how? Why?

7. How have you imagined yourself driving while reading this book? Explain.

8. What, in North American society, is the connection between sexiness, cars, and driving?

9. Do you think driving should be taught in secondary school? Why or why not?

Notes

Notes

EPILOGUE

I would like to thank and salute professional driving teachers everywhere for the responsibility they take on each day with their driving students, and indirectly, for the effect they have on the thousands of people with whom their students will come in contact. With little glory, less remuneration than they deserve, and the challenge of teaching young, tough, "I get it!" minds, they are invaluable. I hope this book will assist them in their important work.

On a more personal note, as I researched and wrote this book, I became immersed in the fragile intricacy of what I can only refer to as "insane" traffic. Amid the first long drive I had undertaken for some time, I found myself experiencing a heightened sensitivity to elements around me. Driving at night in a storm, on a crowded, winding two-lane highway with obscured, alternate lanes blocked off due to construction, my sensitivity to the dangerous driving conducted within inches of my vehicle was close to overwhelming. It was in the midst of a few seconds of near panic that I realized that the time spent researching, speaking about, and preoccupied with accident and fatality statistics had affected my psyche. I was unnerved at the wheel of a vehicle for the first time (without there being an accident to avoid) in many, many years.

In the moment, I knew I had to snap out of it but there was no place to pull over and the diminished highway was pitch-dark and covered with a soup-thick layer of fog. So, I did what I could. I performed a quick mental exercise to force myself to renew my focus (and breathing exercises to relax). This enabled me to drive another 80 miles along the unsupervised, crowded, and competitive truck-versus-car and car-versus-truck speedway until it was safe to pull over and stop. Then, even though I was on a tight schedule, I took time to settle and relegate certain emotions to their rightful place.

I share this with the reader to impress upon him or her that the use of mind and imagination (visualization) when learning anything, let alone the points in this book, is very powerful and exceptionally fortifying of new and stabilizing thinking and actions. On that frightening drive, I reverted to a self-focusing and "centering" exercise commonly used by super-athletes, first responders, NASCAR drivers and others whose performance cannot be compromised, even for a second.

High achievers have long used visualizations and other mental self-management techniques to improve performance. These techniques can assist drivers of all ages to learn how to enhance performance and to settle and focus in a crisis. Drive with your mind—in more ways than one. If you get into trouble, use mental techniques to redirect your thinking and emotions. This life-saving and life-enriching skill is yet another that should be taught to all of us in grade school on into adulthood, not just with respect to driving but with respect to living in general. It is especially important if we are expected to continue to function in a boisterous modern arena unbefitting the sane simplicity of our human hearts and minds.

APPENDIX
Recommendations

A. Beginning Drivers

1. Take a legitimate, formal driving instruction course, ideally one given the stamp of approval by your school.

2. Have another student or friend take the driving course with you. Provide constructive feedback to each other about what you perceive as being possible problem areas related to focus.

3. Start and keep a journal for your first year or more of driving. Note your reactions, the reactions of others, and areas in which your driving requires some ongoing attention and practice.

4. Organize "Driver Awareness" programs at your school. If this is *absolutely impossible*, organize one outside of the school.

5. If you are forming a group outside your school, find a parent or parents who will participate in the group.

6. Become familiar with what internal and external distractions trigger you.

7. Ask what distractions your learning partner might want to become aware of and watch for. Ask what "kind of" driver your co-learner's parents represent.

8. Ask your driving instructor how he or she maintains focus when driving alone and when driving with students.

9. Discuss how dangerously distracting it is to be under the influence of any and all drugs, including alcohol, when one is at the wheel of a car.

10. Discuss how much control you have over your well-being and life when someone else is in any way intoxicated while he or she is driving a car.

11. Learn the rules of the road—the signage and symbols that exist to both guide drivers and to save drivers. It is too little to memorize the rules just to pass a test. In a crunch, you will need to understand road and highway symbols *instantly* in order to avoid an accident.

12. Discuss the no-going-back consequence of ignoring single and double lines when you become impatient behind a slow-moving car.

13. With friends and other students, talk about and adopt a zero-tolerance approach to aggressive and

(all) irresponsible driving. Make a list of what you regard as "aggressive" and "risky" driving.

B. Adult Drivers

1. If you are a parent of young adolescents, begin NOW to encourage their school to include some kind of solid program on "Driver Awareness". Form one if the school cannot do so.

2. Review the driver's handbook about twice a year. Have friends grill you on signage and other driving guides and warnings.

3. Adopt a zero-tolerance policy for aggressive driving.

4. Talk about driver-passenger communication—especially verbal "driver put-downs" and how they leak into one's driving under pressure.

5. Discuss ground rules for driving together as a couple. If the rules do not work, do not drive together. If the situation becomes heated, have the driver stop the vehicle in a safe and populated location and remove yourself from the car.

6. If you have experienced an aggressive-defensive dynamic when driving with someone you know, avoid driving with them.

7. Become familiar with what internal and external distractions trigger you.

8. Get together with a group of friends to discuss your driving weaknesses and strengths, as well as areas that everyone might need to brush up on. Start a movement based on responsible driving.

9. If you saw yourself in this book more than twice, discuss the circumstances with a friend, spouse or relative.

10. After reading and perhaps re-reading this book, highlight your driving idiosyncrasies or bad habits.

11. Start a driving journal to both help you to "de-habit-uate" your driving, as well as to note the degree to which you are paying attention to and improving on your areas of driving weakness.

12. Parents and student drivers tend to set each other off. If a parent is teaching his or her adolescent to drive, it is up to the parent to ensure emotions remain in check. If this is not possible, the student driver should learn with a professional.

13. It should go without saying that no adult should drive under the influence of any drug, including alcohol. Adopt a zero-tolerance policy and model this behavior for your children and other young relatives.

C. Additional Ways to Increase Driver Competency

1. Encourage your school, or parents and school, to invite retired or active professional drivers and trainers to give a presentation.

2. If you are able to do so, take a short day or weekend race-training course yourself. Or, send one driver and have him or her report back on what she or he has learned.

3. Drive with parents of friends and with teachers to ascertain and critique their styles.

4. In the first year for new drivers and periodically thereafter, drive with and for the best driver you know—for short jaunts in urban settings and for short highway drives.

5. Get a summer or part-time job as a training chauffeur.

Selected Bibliography

Abbott A. News: "City Living Marks the Brain". *Nature* 474 (2011):429. doi:10.1038/474429a.

Apicella CL, Marlowe FW, Fowler JH, Christakis NA. "Social Networks and Cooperation in Hunter-Gatherers". *Nature* 481 (2012): 497-502. doi:10.1038/nature10736.

Asbridge M, Hayden JA, Cartwright JL. "Acute Cannabis Consumption and Motor Vehicle Collision Risk: Systematic Review of Observational Studies and Meta-Analysis". *British Medical Journal* (2012) 344:e536. doi:10.1135/bmj.e536.

Berman M. "Teen Drivers Most Likely to Crash in First Month of Solo Driving". *Washington Post,* October 15, 2011.

Beullens K, Roe K, Van den Bulck J. "Excellent Gamer, Excellent Driver? The Impact of Adolescents' Video Game Playing on Driving Behavior: a Two-Wave Panel Study". *Accident Analysis and Prevention* 43, no. 1 (2011):58-65.

Beck KH, Wang MQ, Mitchell MM. "Concerns, Dispositions and Behaviors of Aggressive Drivers: What do Self-identified Aggressive Drivers Believe about Traffic Safety?". *Journal of Safety Research* 37, no. 2 (2006):159-165.

Benson H, Klipper M. *The Relaxation Response.* HarperCollins, New York, 1975.

Centers for Disease Control and Prevention. "Teen Drivers: Fact Sheet". Accessed March 01, 2012. http://www.cdc.gov/Motorvehiclesafety/Teen_Drivers/teendrivers_factsheet.html.

Choi E-H. "Crash Factors in Intersection-Related Crashes: An On-Scene Perspective". *U.S. Department of Transportation, National Highway Traffic Safety Administration* (September 2010). DOT HS 811 366. www.nhtsa.gov.

Connel D, Joint M. "Driver Aggression". *AAA Foundation for Traffic Safety*, Washington, 1996.

Dahl R. "Heavy Traffic Ahead: Car Culture Accelerates". *Environmental Health Perspectives*, 113 no.4 (2005):A238-245.

Dahlen ER, Edwards BD, Tubre T, Zyphur MJ, Warren CR. "Taking a Look behind the Wheel: An Investigation into the Personality Predictors of Aggressive Driving." *Accident Analysis and Prevention* 45 (2012):1-9.

Davies, GM, Patel D. "The Influence of Car and Driver Stereotypes on Attributions of Vehicle Speed, Position on the Road and Culpability in Road Accident Scenario". *Legal and Criminological Psychology* 10, no.1 (2005):45-62. doi:10.1348/135532504X15394

Deaux KK. "Honking at the Intersection: a Replication and Extension". *Journal of Social Psychology* 84, no.1 (1971):159-60.

Deffenbacher JL, Deffenbacher DM, Lynch RS, Richards TL. "Anger, Aggression, and Risky Behavior: a Comparison of High and Low Anger Drivers". *Behavioral Research and Therapy* 41, no. 6 (2003):701-718.

Dingus TA, Klauer SG, Neale VL, Petersen A, Lee Sudweeks J, Perez MA, Hankey J, Ramsey D, Gupta S, Bucher C, Doerzaph ZR, Jermelan J, Knipling RR. "The 100-Car Naturalistic Driving Study Phase II—Results of the 100-Car Field Experiment". *U.S. Department of Transportation, National Highway Traffic Safety Administration (NHTSA)*, 2006. DOT HS 810 593.

Dula CS, Adams CL, Miesner MT, Leonard RL. "Examining Relationships between Anxiety and Dangerous Driving". *Accident Analysis and Prevention* 42 (2010):2050-2056.

Feldman G, Greeson J, Renna M, Robbins-Monteith K. "Mindfulness Predicts Less Texting while Driving among Young Adults: Examining Attention- and Emotion-Regulation Motives as Potential Mediators". *Personality and Individual Differences* 51 (2011):856-861.

Gooderman M. "When Cars Get Really Smart, They Start Talking to the Road." *Globe and Mail*, February 17, 2012.

Greaves SP, Ellison AB. "Personality, Risk Aversion and Speeding: an Empirical Investigation". *Accident Analysis and Prevention* 43, no. 6 (2011):2200-2208.

Griggs, B. " 'Augmented-reality Windshields and the Future of Driving", *CNN Innovations*, January 13,

2012. http://whatsnext.blogs.cnn.com/2012/01/13/augmented-reality-and-the-future-of-driving/

Harris PB, Houston JM. "Recklessness in Context: Individual and Situational Correlates to Aggressive Driving". *Environment and Behavior* 42, no. 1 (2010) SAGE Publications 10.1177/0013916508325234.

Gross, D. "Look, No Hands! The Driverless Future of Driving is Here", *CNN Innovations*, February 22, 2012. http://whatsnext.blogs.cnn.com/2012/02/22/the-sci-fi-future-of-driving-its-already-here/

Harris PG, Houston JM. "Recklessness in Context. Individual and Situational Correlates to Aggressive Driving". *Environment and Behavior* 42 (2010): 44-60.

Hemenway D, Vriniotis M, Miller M. Is an Armed Society a Polite Society? Guns and Road Rage." *Accident Analysis and Prevention* 38, no. 4 (2006):687-695.

Hennessey D. "The Interaction of Person and Situation within the Driving Environment: Daily Hassles, Traffic Congestion, Driver Stress, Aggression, Vengeance, and Past Performance" Ph.D. dissertation, York University, Toronto, Ontario, April 1999.

Hennessy DA, Wiesenthal DL. "Age and Vengeance as Predictors of Mild Driver Aggression". *Violence and Victims* 19, no. 4 (2004):469-477.

Hosking S, Young K, Regan M. "The effects of text messaging on young novice driver performance". *Monash University Accident Research Centre*, February 2006, Report No: 246.

International Traffic Safety Data and Analysis Group Annual Report 2010. http://www.trb.org/Main/Blurbs/ OECD_International_Traffic_Safety_Data_and_ Analysi_164620.aspx

Johnson MB, McKnight S. "Warning Drivers about Potential Congestion as a Means to Reduce Frustration-Driven Aggressive Driving". *Traffic Injury Prevention* 10, no. 4 (2009):354-360.

Johnson TD. "Distracted Driving: Stay Focused while on the Road". *American Public Health Association,* February 2012. Available at www.thenationshealth.org

Joint M. "Road Rage". *The Automobile Association Foundation for Traffic Safety*, Washington, 1995.

Just MA, Keller TA, Cynkar J. "A Decrease in Brain Activation Associated with Driving when Listening to Someone Speak". *Brain Research* (2008) 1205: 70-80. doi:10.1016/j.brainres.2007.12.075/

Ker K, Roberts I, Collier T, Renton F, Bunn F. Post-license driver education for the prevention of road traffic crashes. *Cochrane Database of Systematic Reviews* 2003 (3): CD003734.

Kopits E, Cropper M. "Traffic Fatalities and Economic Growth". *Accident Analysis and Prevention* 37, no.5 (2005):169-177.

Ian R, Irene K. " School based driver education for the prevention of traffic crashes". *Cochrane Database of Systematic Reviews* 2001 (3): CD003201.

Lanier J. *You Are Not a Gadget.* New York. Richard A. Knopf, 2010.

Larue GS, Rakotonirainy A, Pettitt AN. "Driving Performance Impairments Due to Hypovigilance on Monotonous Roads". *Accident Analysis and Prevention* 43 (2011):2037-2046.

Lefkovitz M, Blake R, Mouton JS. "Status Factors in Violation of Traffic Signals". *Journal of Abnormal and Social Psychology* 51, no.3 (1955):704-706.

Lennon A, Watson B. "Teaching them a Lesson? A Qualitative Exploration of Underlying Motivations for Driver Aggression". *Accident Analysis and Prevention* 43 (2011):2200-2208.

Lerner, BH. "Drunk Driving, Distracted Driving, Moralism and Public Health". *New England Journal of Medicine* 365, no.10 (2011):880-881.

Licht A. "Social Norms and the Law: Why People Obey the Law". *Review of Law & Economics* 4, no.3 (2009), Article 3, doi:10.2202/1555-5879.1232. http://www.faculty.idc.ac.il/licht/papers.htm

Markoff J. "Collision in the Making Between Self-Driving Cars and How the World Works". *Globe and Mail*, January 23, 2012.

Masten S, Foss R, Marshall D. "Graduated Driver Licensing and Fatal Crashes involving 16 to 19-Year-Old Drivers". *Journal of American Medical Association* 306, no. 10 (2011):1098- 1103.

McCartt A, Teoh E. "Strengthening Driver Licensing Systems for Teenaged Drivers". *Journal of American Medical Association* 306, no. 10 (2011):1142-1143.

McKnight C E, Mouskos K, Kamga C et al. "New York Metropolitan Transportation Council (NYMTC) Pedestrian Safety in the NYMTC Region". *Institute for Transportation Systems*, City University of New York, 2007.

Morris J D. "Driver Violence Tied to Crashes: Federal Report Asks Study of Uncontrollable Behavior". *New York Times*, March 01, 1968.

Mueller J. "A False Sense of Security". *Regulation* 27, no.3 (2004):42-46.

Norton PD. "Jaywalking and the Invention of the Motor Age Street". *Technology and Culture* 48, no.2 (2004):331-245.

Olson RL, Hanowski RJ, Hickman JS, Bocanegra J. "Driver Distraction in Commercial Vehicle Operations". *U.S. Department of Transportation, Federal Motor Carrier Safety Administration*, Report No FMCSA-RRR-09-042, 2009.

Ozkan T, Lajunen T, Parker D, Sumer N, Summala H. Symmetric Relationship between Self and Others in Aggressive Driving across Gender and Countries". *Traffic Injury Prevention* 11, no. 3 (2010):228-39.

Parry MH. *Aggression on the Road*. London: Tavistock Publications, 1968.

Peltzman S. "The Effects of Automobile Safety Regulation". *Journal of Political Economy* 83, no. 4 (1975):677-726.

Preston CH, Harris S. "Psychology of Drivers in Traffic Accidents". *Journal of Applied Psychology* 49, no. 4 (1965):244-248. doi:10.1037/h0022453.

Ransom, K. "Michigan Readies For Tougher Teen Driving Laws. Studies Show Driving Restrictions Can Save

Lives", February 12, 2011. http://autos.aol.com/article/teen-driving-laws/

Regan M., Hallet C. Gordon C. "Driver distraction and driver inattention: definition, relationship and taxonomy". *Accident Analysis and Prevention* 43 (2011):1771-1781.

Roberts LD, Indermaur DW. "The "Homogamy" of Road Rage Revisited". *Violence and Victims* 23, no. 6 (2008):758-772.

Rowden P, Matthews G, Watson B, Biggs H. The Relative Impact of Work-related Stress, Life Stress and Driving Environment Stress on Driving Outcomes. *Accident Analysis and Prevention* (2011). doi:10.1016/j.aap.2011.02.004.

Rudin-Brown CM. "The Effect of Driver Eye Height on Speed Choice, Lane-Keeping, and Car-Following Behavior: Results of Two Driving Simulator Studies". *Traffic Injury Prevention* 7, no. 4 (2006):365-372.

Russell KF, Vandermeer B, Hartling L. "Graduated Driver Licensing for Reducing Motor Vehicle Crashes among Young Drivers". Cochrane Database of Systematic Reviewers (2011) 10:CD003300.

Schneider RJ., Ryznar RM., Khattack AJ. "An Accident Waiting to Happen: A Spatial Approach to Proactive Pedestrian Planning". *Accident Analysis and Prevention* 36, no. 2 (2004):193-211.

Shelden HC. "Prevention, the Only Cure for Head Injuries Resulting from Automobile Accidents". *Journal of American Medical Association* 159, no. 10 (1955):981-986.

Silk JB. News & Views. "The Path to Sociality". *Nature* 479 (2011):182-183.

Simons-Morton BG, Ouimet MC, Zhang A, Klauer SE, Lee SE, Wang J, Chen R, Albert P, Dingus TA. "The Effect of Passengers and Risk-Taking Friends on Risky Driving and Crashes/Near Crashes Among Novice Teenagers". *Journal of Adolescent Health* 49 (2011):587-593.

Sivak M. "Homicide Rate as a Predictor of Traffic Fatality Rate". *Traffic Injury Prevention* 10, no. 6 (2009):511-512.

Smart RG, Sotduto G, Adlaf EM, Mnn RE, Sharpley JM. " Road rage victimization among adolescents". *Journal of Adolescent Health* 41, no. 3 (2007):277-282.

Sobel RS, Nesbitt T. "Automobile Safety Regulation and the Incentive to Drive Recklessly: Evidence from NASCAR". *Southern Economic Journal* 74, no. 1 (2004):71-84.

Steinberg L. "Editorial: Adolescents' Risky Driving in Context". *Journal of Adolescent Health* 49 (2011): 557-558.

Stephens AN, Groeger JA. "Anger-Congruent Behaviour Transfers across Driving Situations". *Cognition & Emotion* 25, no. 8 (2011): 1423-1438.

Strayer DL, Drews FA, Crouch DJ. A comparison of the Cell Phone Driver and the Drunk Driver. *Human Factors* 48, no. 2 (Summer 2006): 381-391.

Tasca L. "A Review of the Literature on Aggressive Driving Research". *Ontario Advisory Group on Safe Driving Secretariat Road User Safety Branch*. Ontario Ministry of Transportation Canada 2000.

Taubman-Ben-Ari O. "The effects of Positive Emotion Priming on Self-Reported Reckless Driving". *Accident Analysis and Prevention* (2011), doi: 10.1016/j. aap.2011.09.039.

U.S. Department of Transportation. "Traffic Safety Facts 2006: A Compilation of Motor Vehicle Crash Data from the Fatality Analysis Reporting System and the General Estimates System". *National Highway Traffic Safety Administration* (NHTSA). DOT HS 810 818.

U.S. Department of Transportation. "Traffic Safety Facts 2009 (Early Edition). A Compilation of Motor Vehicle Crash Data from the Fatality Analysis Reporting System and the General Estimates System". *National Highway Traffic Safety Administration (NHTSA).* DOT HS 811 402.

U.S. Department of Transportation. " Overview of Results From the International Traffic Safety Data and Analysis Group Survey on Distracted Driving Data Collection and Reporting. *National Highway Traffic Safety Administration*, 2010. DOT HS 811 404.

Walton D, Thomas A. "Measuring Perceived Risk: Self-Reported and Actual Hand Positions of SUV and Car Drivers". *Transportation Research Part F: Traffic Psychology and Behavior* 10, no. 3 (2007):201-207.

Wasielewski P. Evans L. "Do Drivers of Small Cars Take More Risks in Everyday Life?" *Risk Analysis* 5, no. 1 (1985):25-32.

Weaver J. News: "Amygdala at the Centre of Your Social Network". *Nature* 26 December 2010. doi:10.1038/news.2010.699.

White CB, Caird JK. "The Blind Date: the Effects of Change Blindness, Passenger Conversation and Gender on Looked-but-Failed-to-See (LBFTS) Errors". *Accident Analysis and Prevention* 42 (2010):1822-1830.

Whitlock, FA. *Death on the Road: a Study in Social Violence*. London: Tavistock Publications, 1968.

Wickens CM, Mann RE, Stoduto G, Butters JE, Ialomiteanu A, Smart RG. "Does Gender Moderate the Relationship between Driver Aggression and its Risk Factors?" *Accident Analysis and Prevention* 45, no.2 (2012):10-18.

Wickens CM, Wiesenthal DL, Flora DB, Flett GL. "Understanding Driver Anger and Aggression: Attributional Theory in the Driving Environment". *Journal of Experimental Psychology, Applied* 17, no.4 (2011):354-370.

World Health Organization and Bank. "World Report on Road Traffic Injury Prevention 2004". http://www.who.int/violence_injury_prevention/publications/road_traffic/world_report/en/

World Health Organization. "Global Plan for the Decade of Action for Road Safety 2011—2020". http://www.who.int/roadsafety/decade_of_action/plan/en/index.html

World Health Organization. "Global Status Report on Road Safety 2009". http://www.who.int/violence_injury_prevention/road_safety _status /2009/en/index.html

Williams AF. Krychenko SY, Retting, R. "Characteristics of Speeders". *Journal of Safety Research* 37, no. 3 (2006):227-32.

Yazawa H. "Effects of Inferred Social Status and a Beginning Driver's Sticker upon Aggression of Drivers in Japan". *Psychology Report* 94 (2004):1215-1220.

BRING THE AUTHOR TO YOU!

Dr. Lauren is currently working with school boards to introduce driving programs to new and prospective drivers. To introduce a program at your school or to book Dr. Lauren for an entertaining and informative presentation on "NON-CRASH" driving and performance, email your request to:

speakers.socialresponsibility@gmail.com or
drlauren@drlaurenspeaks.com

or call:
Toronto, Canada, 416-481-2768

See also www.drlaurenspeaks.com

Also by Dr. Lauren

LAUGHING in the Face of CHANGE—
A Blueprint for a Return to Joy!

ESSENTIAL ADJUSTMENTS—
Showing Up for the New Millennium

It's OUR Sanity!!
Conscious Living in an Unconscious World

HARD LESSONS—
Understanding and Addressing the Unprecedented
Danger Facing Today's Youth

Shooter in the Sky—
The Inner World of Children who Kill

Millenial Madness—Tips and Truths
from a Therapist Managing Madness

Books may be purchased at:
www.drlaurenenterprises.com
or your favorite bookstore.

Index

About the Author

The author and her navigator

Dr. Lauren, as she has long been known, is, among other things, a television commentator, international speaker and educator-entertainer, therapist, career and life strategist, performance specialist and hands-on activist for the homeless. She has performed competitively in over five sports and is a consultant, worldwide, to professional athletes and teams, as well as to CEOs, middle and senior management, corporate populations, and politicians. She is also a placing race-car driver and has driven sundry vehicles in red-hot war zones. A prolific author, Dr. Lauren has been the recipient of numerous writing, service and academic awards. Among other degrees, she earned her doctorate in psychology summa cum laude at the Southern California University graduate school for professional studies. Dr. Lauren resides, most often, in Toronto, Canada.

Dr. Lauren is available for speaking engagements on this and other topics.

In addition, her national one-woman show, "Road Beings", begins in the fall of 2012.

LEARN MORE about Dr. Lauren at
www.drlaurenspeaks.com
or email speakers.socialresponsibility@gmail.com

D0287041

The Real World?

THE REAL WORLD?

Michel Tremblay

Talonbooks • Vancouver • 1988

copyright ©1988 Michel Tremblay

translation copyright ©1988 John Van Burek and
Bill Glassco

published with assistance from the Canada Council

Talonbooks
201/1019 East Cordova Street
Vancouver, British Columbia
Canada V6A 1M8

LEDL
CIRC
PQ
3919.2
.T73
V 7313

This book was typeset in Garth by Pièce de Résistance
Graphics, and printed by Hignell Printing Ltd.

Printed in Canada

First printing: October 1988

All rights in and to this work are retained by the
author, and interested persons are requested to apply to
his agent, L'Agence Artistique et Littéraire, 839,
Sherbrooke Est, Suite 2, Montréal, Québec H2L 1K6.

First published by Les Editions Leméac Inc., Montréal,
Québec.

Canadian Cataloguing in Publication Data

Tremblay, Michel, 1943-
  [Le vrai monde? English]
  The real world?

  Translation of: Le vrai monde?
  ISBN 0-88922-260-6

  I. Title.   II. Title: Le vrai monde?
English.
PS8539.R47V713 1988   C842'.54   C88-091495-5
PQ3919.2.T73V713 1988

ACM 4566

Le Vrai Monde? was first performed at le Théâtre du
Rideau Vert in Montréal, Québec, on April 15, 1987,
with the following cast:

Madeleine II	Angèle Coutu
Madeleine I	Rita Lafontaine
Claude	Patrice Coquereau
Alex I	Gilles Renaud
Alex II	Raymond Bouchard
Mariette I	Sylvie Ferlatte
Mariette II	Julie Vincent

Directed by André Brassard
Assisted by Lou Fortier
Costumes by François Barbeau
Set Design by Martin Ferland
Lighting by Claude Accolas

The Real World? was first performed in English at
Tarragon Theatre in Toronto, Ontario, on May 24, 1988,
with the following cast:

Madeleine II	Shirley Douglas
Madeleine I	Clare Coulter
Claude	Michael McManus
Alex I	Graeme Campbell
Alex II	Ken James
Mariette I	Julie A. Stewart
Mariette II	Shannon Lawson

Directed by Bill Glassco
Costumes by François Barbeau
Set Design by André Henault
Lighting by Jeffrey Dallas

The living room is empty.
We hear the third movement of Mendelsohn's fifth symphony.
MADELEINE II enters; she seems troubled.
She goes to the door, pulls the curtain, and looks outside.
She crosses the living room again and goes out.
We hear a popular song from the mid-sixties.

CLAUDE and ALEX I enter. CLAUDE carries a leather briefcase, his father a small suitcase.

CLAUDE:
Looks like you never left the dirt roads. I've never seen such a filthy car . . .

ALEX I:
Nonsense! When you were a kid, my car was always that dirty . . . There weren't many paved roads in the forties . . . But of course, you don't notice things like that . . . You've always got your nose buried in books, how would you know what my car looks like . . .

MADELEINE I comes in from the kitchen. She is dressed like MADELEINE II, but simpler, more "realistically."

MADELEINE I:
Home already, Alex? I didn't expect you 'til tomorrow . . .   *She is visibly uneasy; coldly:*
Hello, Claude . . .

CLAUDE:
Hi . . .

He kisses his mother awkwardly.

7

ALEX I:
Gee, I can tell you're thrilled to see me . . . No kiss for hubby? You haven't seen me for a whole week. Claude, you see him almost every day . . . worry about him later . . .

He lifts her off the ground, gives her a big kiss on the cheek.

MADELEINE I:
Alex, for God's sake . . .

ALEX I:
Mmmm, smells good . . . I mean . . . you smell good, the whole house smells good . . .

MADELEINE I:
Life goes on, even when you're away.

She goes out.

ALEX I:
Something happen while I was gone?

CLAUDE:
I don't know . . . don't think so . . . Anyway, I haven't been here for at least a week . . . I don't hang around all the time . . .

ALEX I:
It wasn't that way when you moved out . . . You always came home to eat with your mother . . .

CLAUDE:
That was two years ago . . .

ALEX I:
Two years! Already! You sure?

CLAUDE:
Believe it or not, I've learned how to cook myself a steak, and the peas that go with it . . .

Silence.

ALEX I:
So, how's the new job?

CLAUDE:
It's okay.

ALEX I:
That's all you've got to say?

CLAUDE:
Listen, Papa, I've got the most boring job in the world. Just because it's a new one doesn't make it any better.

ALEX I:
If you'd listened to me . . .

CLAUDE:
Oh please, let's not start that again . . . We've been over this a hundred times, it's pointless . . . I have no interest in roaming the countryside year in, year out, flogging insurance with a smile on my face and a hatful of jokes . . . especially under the protection of my famous father . . . Can you see us two travelling together? We'd have killed each other in two weeks!

ALEX I:
You'd be on your own in no time . . . build your own clientele, like me.

CLAUDE:
Papa, please, you're giving me the creeps!

ALEX I:
Well I still think you'd be happier that way than spending your life strapped to a machine that drives you nuts . . . And you'd see the country! At least I've spent my life in the open air. And I've had fun! I'm not bored up the ass eight hours a day in some printing shop that stinks to high heaven!

CLAUDE:
>   I won't be strapped to that machine much longer . . .

ALEX I:
>   You still dream of being a writer. You make a living,
>   but you're stuck in a job you don't like . . . and you
>   dream of starving to death in a job that'll never
>   support you . . . I'll never understand you . . .

CLAUDE:
>   What else is new . . .

>   *ALEX I looks at his son for a few seconds. We can
>   feel the tension mount.*

ALEX I:
>   You still carry your little briefcase, like an
>   intellectual? What do you keep in there? Your
>   lunch?   *CLAUDE lowers his eyes.*   Your lunch
>   and your manuscripts . . . When can we expect the
>   great revelation? Eh? The third Tuesday next month?
>   Mind you, if it's poetry, don't bother. I get enough of
>   that from those jerks plunking their guitars in every
>   hotel in the province . . . How come all you people
>   are plunking guitars all of a sudden? It's an epidemic!
>   I just saw another one, Saturday night in
>   Saint-Jérôme. Jesus-Christ, even Felix Leclerc's not
>   that boring.

CLAUDE:
>   Don't worry . . . What I write about has nothing to do
>   with guitars . . .

ALEX I:
>   That's a relief . . . I guess.   *He laughs.*   I know
>   you well enough to know that whatever you write
>   isn't gonna make me do handstands . . .

CLAUDE:
>   Then don't ask me why I don't show it to you . . .

MADELEINE I returns clutching a manuscript.
CLAUDE turns away slightly.

ALEX I:
A roast of veal? A chicken?

MADELEINE I:
Roast of veal.   *Ironically.*   Claude's so fond of
that . . .

ALEX I: *to CLAUDE*
That reminds me . . . Go look in the trunk of the
car . . . I've got a whole bag of corn . . . first of the
year . . . It's beautiful, it's young, it's tender . . . Just
like me!

MADELEINE I rolls her eyes to heaven.

MADELEINE I:
Spare us the travelling salesman jokes . . .

ALEX I:
It's my travelling salesman jokes that pay for your
roast of veal, Madeleine!   *MADELEINE I and
CLAUDE look at each other.*   Okay, I'm going to
take a bath . . . I've a hunch I smell like team
work . . .   *He laughs.*   Don't miss me too
much . . .

He goes out.
Silence.
*MADELEINE I lays the manuscript on the coffee
table.*

CLAUDE:
Have you read it?

MADELEINE I:
Yes.   *Silence.*   How could you do that . . . ? I
was so ashamed reading it, Claude . . . I felt so . . .
ugly.

CLAUDE:
Ugly?

MADELEINE I: *sharply*
That's not me! That's not how I am! That woman,
even if she has my name, is nothing like me! And I
don't want her to be. How dare you give her my
name, Claude!

CLAUDE:
But Mama, it's a character in a play . . . Nothing says
it's you . . .

MADELEINE I:
Claude! What do you take me for? You describe our
living room down to the last detail! The furniture, the
curtains, the frayed carpet in front of the door, the
Admiral T.V . . . It takes place right here, in our
house, how do you expect me not to think you
wanted to describe us in those characters! I
recognized my dress, Claude, I recognized my hairdo,
but I didn't recognize myself!

> *We hear the beginning of the third movement of
> Mendelsohn's fifth symphony.*
> *MADELEINE II enters; she seems troubled. She is
> dressed like MADELEINE I.*
> *MADELEINE I picks up the manuscript.*

MADELEINE I:
What's in here is not me!

> *MADELEINE II goes to the window, pulls the
> curtains and looks out.*

MADELEINE I:
That's not me!

> *MADELEINE II crosses the room again in silence,
> and goes out.*

MADELEINE I:

That's not even the music I listen to! The music you put in there, I don't know it. And I don't want to! The music I listen to is simple, it's easy to remember, I can sing along with it. You hear what's playing on the kitchen radio? Well, that's what I like. Not your . . . your . . .

CLAUDE:

Mendelsohn . . .

MADELEINE I:

Your Mendelsohn that you've found God knows where . . . from your own taste probably . . . Were you ashamed to put that in your play? I can't understand what you were after! You've made us all ugly, but you've made us listen to music you think is more beautiful, more refined than what we like! You make fools of us, Claude, do you realize that?

CLAUDE:

But I don't. I don't make fools of you. Come and sit next to me. I'll try to explain . . .

MADELEINE I:

I don't want explanations, it's too late for that, the harm's been done! You have no idea how much you've hurt me . . . *Silence.* How can you think . . . that I ever thought such things, that I ever said . . . such monstrous things to your father!

CLAUDE:

I know you never said them . . . that's why I wrote them. Mama, there are things in this house that should have been dealt with a long time ago, that have never been settled . . .

MADELEINE I:

Who are you to decide what's to be settled between your father and me . . .

13

ALEX II enters with an enormous bouquet of flowers.

ALEX II:
   Madeleine! Madeleine, are you there?

CLAUDE:
   That's not what I was trying to do . . . I wasn't trying
   to settle them, but I wanted those things to be said
   once and for all.

   *MADELEINE II comes back in, her arms folded
   across her chest, like the real MADELEINE.*

MADELEINE II:
   I've been waiting for you for two days. Flowers won't
   settle a thing.

ALEX II:
   Okay, what is it this time . . . You know I had a long
   way to go . . .

   MADELEINE II looks him straight in the eye.

MADELEINE II:
   Alex, I know exactly where you've been . . .

ALEX II:
   What's that supposed to mean? I told you, this time I
   might have to go all the way to Sept Îsles . . . Sept
   Îsles, Madeleine, that's not next door!

MADELEINE II:
   No, but Sorel is right around the corner, isn't it?
   ALEX II is flummoxed. Silence.   Sept Îsles! I've
   known for ages you don't cover the whole province of
   Quebec by yourself. In the beginning . . . in the
   beginning, when I was young, I believed you, I
   thought you went everywhere, that you were the only
   one out there . . . I was even naive enough to think
   your company depended almost entirely on you.
   When you talked about your job you made yourself

14

sound so important, I was convinced that if you disappeared your company'd go bankrupt . . . I loved you that much . . .

ALEX II:
Why the past tense? You don't love me anymore? I still love you . . .

She looks at him a few seconds before replying.

MADELEINE II:
Indeed, sometimes just to get through the day, I tell myself you must love me, in your way.

ALEX II:
Madeleine, what's wrong with you lately, you seem distant . . . but I've been telling myself it's not serious, it'll pass . . .

MADELEINE II:
Alex, I really don't feel like listening to your excuses . . . But . . . I'm fed up being taken for a fool . . . I've started to take myself for a fool, and that, Alex, I won't do . . .

ALEX II:
Excuses . . . for what?

MADELEINE II:
Everything! The lies, the cheating, the manipulation, your specialty, which only I couldn't see . . . I believed you for so long, and I was content to believe you . . .

ALEX II:
For Chrissake, are you going to start accusing me too, of always being happy! It's bad enough when the kids make cracks all the time! Sure, I manipulate, sure, I want people to like me, and sure, I do everything so they will, but that doesn't make me a bastard!

MADELEINE II:

It's not people I want to talk about, Alex . . . You can do what you want with them, that's your job. It's your job to seduce them with your stupid jokes and dirty stories so they'll sign their names to a contract that's likely going to screw them.

ALEX II:

That's how you see my job . . .

MADELEINE II:

That's how you talk about it . . . You ever listen to yourself? You ever stop to think about the stupid things you say in one day? Jokes are fine, Alex, even dirty ones, but not all day long. When we were first married I said to myself, that's okay, he wants to make me laugh, it'll pass . . . until I realized you were always that way, and you probably always would be . . . I loved you too much to admit you got on my nerves . . . or I wanted to love you too much. I was the only one in the family to find something resembling love, and I did everything, everything I could not to lose it . . . I even stayed blind to what you were doing . . .

ALEX II:

But what did I do? All my life I've slaved for you and the kids . . . You've had nothing to complain about, never! Nobody has! Sure, I travelled a lot, but when I came home we had fun! We've had fun in this house for years, Madeleine, we don't kill each other like everyone else in your family, and you want to complain! Christ, does everyone in your family have to suffer? Would you rather I knocked you around after I'd had a few? Like your brother-in-law? When the kids were small their friends would love to have had me for a father, I was like Santa Claus with Mariette and Claude! Did you want me to be a boogie man they'd run away from when I got home? I gave those kids presents, Madeleine, not bruises! I came back to town like a ray of sunshine, and the whole

damn street was happy to see me! Everyone envied you, so don't tell me I made you miserable!

MADELEINE II:

Alex, I know you've got answers for everything . . . That's why I avoid these arguments . . . You're a smooth talker, that's how you make your living and put food on the table, you know how to control a conversation . . . Next to you we're helpless, defenceless . . . We let you win because even if we argue for hours sooner or later you'll get us with some devious trick or joke . . . See, you've turned the conversation already. I was determined to try and talk to you calmly, to tell you calmly that I know what you've done to me, and you've got me all mixed up already . . . I feel like going back to the kitchen to finish supper, pretending I know nothing, that I'm ignorant and happy again! No question, I was better off when I knew nothing, when my world stopped at the doorstep, and my only worries were that the kids eat properly and be well dressed, and for you to be proud of us when you came home . . . No question . . . When you know nothing, you can't be hurt . . . See that door? . . . That's where my world stopped, Alex, and I was perfectly happy. Perfectly! For . . . I don't know, twenty years. When you were out of my sight, you vanished into thin air, almost ceased to exist . . . You became . . . I don't know . . . Prince Charming on a promotional tour . . . I knew you were off playing the clown to put food in our mouths, but since I never saw you at it, I could imagine whatever I liked. For me you were someone important . . . I admired you! *She sits on the sofa next to MADELEINE I.* Now I'm caught in the middle of a scene I didn't plan, and I don't know how to continue.

MADELEINE I:

Did you ever consider, Claude, that I'm too proud to admit such things . . . I'd rather die than say those things to your father.

ALEX II:
> I've always admired you too . . . *MADELEINE II stiffens on the sofa.* No, no let me finish . . .

MADELEINE II:
> No, Alex . . . I know what you're going to say and I don't want to fall into the trap . . . I'd rather keep you from talking than let myself be fooled again . . .

ALEX II:
> I don't have the right to speak in my own house? Is that it? You're so afraid of being wrong, you're going to keep me from talking! For once I'm about to pay you compliments, real ones, heartfelt, and you're going to plug your ears!

MADELEINE II:
> I don't want your admiration, Alex. It's contemptuous! You admire me like a statue on a shelf, like a tin of Campbell's soup that's handy when you get hungry before bed! You don't admire me, you appreciate the fact I'm always here to wait on you when you come home, that's all. For you this house has never been more than a train station. You only come here waiting to leave again. Convenient, eh? While you were out gallivanting around the province you could always be sure there were three saps waiting patiently, keeping your meals hot, your bed clean, and your slippers under your armchair!

ALEX II:
> I don't recognize you . . .

MADELEINE II:
> I hope not! And I tell you, it'll be a while before you do.

ALEX II:

Listen . . . Let's just calm down . . . I come home happy, with a bouquet of flowers that cost me an arm and a leg . . . We haven't seen each other for over a week . . . I'm eager to get home . . . I walk in, and I find another woman!

MADELEINE II:

Ahah! That's exactly what I wanted to talk about. Thank you. You got us back on the subject without meaning to . . . another woman!

MADELEINE I gets up.

MADELEINE I: *very sharply*

You've got nerve! Making up stories like that just to be interesting! Your father's right. You've always had a . . . warped imagination . . .

CLAUDE:

You'd rather let Papa be right than admit the truth . . .

MADELEINE I:

What truth? Yours? One that you fancy because it's more interesting for your play?

CLAUDE:

Mama . . . there's no point pretending you don't know about Papa . . . Mariette and I have known the truth about him for ages . . .

MADELEINE I:

Well, keep it to yourself! Don't put it on paper! Someone might read it! I don't even admit those things to myself; how do you expect me to tolerate finding them in some play! Now I've read that, I'll never be able to look at your father in the same way. Never thought of that, did you, you just wanted to smear him! To smear us! That scene about other women never took place, and it never will, you hear

19

me? As long as I live I'll keep that scene from happening!

CLAUDE:
I hoped it would do you good . . .

MADELEINE I:
Well, it didn't! It revived something in me that I'd buried forever. Forever, Claude! You've brought back . . . the one thing that almost drove me insane . . . doubt. Thanks to you, I've started to doubt again, and I'll never forgive you!

She leaves the room.

MADELEINE II:
I've never talked to you . . . about other women . . .

ALEX II:
What other women?

MADELEINE II:
Alex, please, don't make this more difficult . . . it's hard enough already. Let's not play games. Everyone in the house knows, Alex. We always have.

ALEX II:
Why do we have to talk about this . . . ?

MADELEINE II:
To get it off my chest, maybe.

ALEX II:
I don't want to talk about these things. It's embarrassing. They're unimportant anyway. Women have always attracted me, you know that . . . I never denied it . . .

MADELEINE II:
You're telling me . . . Every year at Christmas I was terrified . . . A woman couldn't make it through the door without you lunging at her.

ALEX II:
Come off it, Madeleine! Sure, after a few drinks, I'd
get a bit enterprising, but so did all the men!

MADELEINE II:
Sure, with you guys it's always the same. Without a
drink you're shy as calves, but once you've tanked
up, any woman's fair game! Christmas, weddings,
First Communions, any excuse for a party! A few
drinks and you can't keep your hands off, that's your
idea of a party! You don't even try to hide it when
you're pawing your sisters-in-law or your young
cousins. You do it in front of everyone too, roaring
away, making lewd jokes just to show it's not serious.
'Course not! As long as it doesn't go too far, eh? The
drinks give you the freedom to carry on, but you
know you can't go too far. Meanwhile we poor girls
sit there like idiots laughing our heads off 'cause we
don't know what else to do. Because we're so
ashamed. We're ashamed of you guys, so we laugh!
But it's not men in general I want to talk about, it's
you, about what you've been doing all these years
while you were gone; about what I bet you're still
doing, that's what I want to talk about . . .

ALEX II:
What I do when I go out that door is my business,
Madeleine. If something happens at the other end of
the province, what do you care? Look, I'm a
red-blooded man, I've got needs. Sometimes I'm gone
for weeks, and . . . there are women for that,
Madeleine, and you know it! But it's not serious. It
doesn't stop me feeling what I feel for you. And I've
never let you down, I've always . . . When I come
home, Madeleine, you can't say . . . I don't know
how to talk about these things! What you don't know
won't hurt you, why do you want to know
everything?

21

MADELEINE II:

I know enough already, thank you, and it hurts! I've got my pride too, you know! You can't walk all over me like that and not expect me to feel something! You've been laughing at me since the day we got married, Alex. I've had enough!

ALEX II:

I don't laugh at you!

MADELEINE II:

You're laughing at me right now! Because you've no idea how much I know . . . Because you hope I don't know everything! Well, let me tell you a story. Just one, to show you what I've put up with . . . One day someone knocked at the door . . . I opened it. It was a woman, with a little girl in her arms. You know what I'm talking about? *ALEX II turns away.* She said her name was Madame Cantin . . . Does that ring a bell, Alex, Madame Cantin . . . from Sorel?

ALEX II:

She came here?

MADELEINE II:

Years ago. She told me she hadn't seen you for months, that you'd left her without a cent . . .

ALEX II:

You've known each other for years and neither one of you ever told me!

MADELEINE II:

We have our little secrets too, you know . . . How old is she now, that little girl? Must be a teenager. Don't worry, we don't get together behind your back. I don't even know her phone number. But I know she exists, and that's what kills me! Can you imagine how I felt giving her ten dollars out of my purse? Eh? The humiliation! For her as much as for me! Behind the clown, the joker, the professional smoothie, there's a man I don't know, who leads a double life I don't

22

know, and who probably cheats on this second woman with yet a third . . . Is there an end, is there any end, Alex, to your cheating? Have you sown your oats in every city you've worked in? Is there a Madame Cantin in Sept Îsles, another in Drummondville? Do they all have trouble feeding your kids? Madame Cantin called from Sorel this afternoon, Alex . . . Once again you "forgot" to leave her some money . . . And I can't live with this lie any longer.

ALEX II:
That kid's probably not even mine! I got taken for a ride, what else could I do? She meant no more than the others at first, but . . . but one day she said I'd got her pregnant and I believed her . . . I should have dropped her then and there 'cause she'd known lots of men before me, and nothing says that kid was mine . . . But . . . you, you didn't want any more kids, and I felt like it . . . it made me feel good to have another one . . .

MADELEINE II:
Sure, keep it up, it'll be my fault . . .

ALEX II: *cutting her off*
And I've always assumed my responsibilities . . .

MADELEINE II:
You left her repeatedly with no money!

ALEX II:
I didn't have any! It was hard enough feeding the rest of you. I was up against it, Madeleine. There were times I left you without money too! If I didn't have enough for you, how could I give her any? And there aren't any others, at Sept Îsles or Drummondville. She's the only one . . .

MADELEINE II:
You mean she's the only one with kids . . .

ALEX II:

> Some guys should never get married. I found out too
> late I was one of them . . .

MADELEINE II:

> Boy, you sure solve problems fast! Is that why you
> dumped us in the backwoods every summer from
> June to September, and gave us the thrill of your
> presence once in a blue moon . . . You carried on like
> you weren't even married! One helluva life, eh! Every
> year, three months off to go chase skirts! A month
> here, a month there . . . Do you tell them all the same
> thing when they question you? Do you? Do you say
> it's me who's not important, or do I have the honour
> of being queen-mother?

ALEX II:

> What am I supposed to say! You think I was happy all
> those years . . . ?

MADELEINE II:

> Hey, don't expect me to feel sorry for you!

ALEX II:

> Will you let me talk! Okay, it's true . . . I like to sow
> my oats, as you put it . . . But for me it's not
> important . . . It's just . . . it's just a need, it's
> natural . . . something I happen to feel when I'm
> alone on a Saturday night, stuck in some gloomy
> hotel . . . And if it weren't for that kid . . .

MADELEINE II:

> If it weren't for that kid I'd never have known and
> things would have gone on like before 'til the end of
> time, right? Deep down inside, that's your dream,
> isn't it? To be Mr. Wonderful with me while you
> laugh behind my back, as you skip from town to
> town, woman to woman, knowing I'll always be here
> in my fool's paradise, in blissful ignorance, with my
> roast of beef and my apple pie! And in spite of
> everything, that's what I cooked yesterday, a roast of
> beef and an apple pie . . . because that's what you

like . . . But the roast dried up and I couldn't resist the pie. There are two pieces missing . . .

She holds her sides.

ALEX II:
What's wrong? You in pain again?

MADELEINE II:
I can deal with my own pain, thank you . . . Never mind the sympathy. It'll get you no further than your stupid jokes. Now that you know everything, no need to tell you I don't want to go on. I'll never find you funny again, and if you only knew how good that makes me feel! I'll do everything possible to get a divorce, Alex. Even though I know it's going to be long and hard. In the mean time, while you're in Montreal you can find yourself a gloomy hotel; that way you can be sure you won't be bored on Saturday nights . . .

She goes out.
Silence.
ALEX II goes to the telephone.

ALEX II:
Goddamnit! She'll pay for that!

He goes out with the telephone.
MADELEINE I enters.
She is holding a glass of milk.

CLAUDE:
You in pain again?

MADELEINE I:
You had no business talking about that either. But I suppose there's no point telling you that. There's just one thing I want you to know, Claude. I won't stay long, I'm going to disappear into my kitchen, as I always do. It's a roast of veal this time, just to be different from your play . . . but don't worry, there's

an apple pie . . .   *Silence*   I want to tell you
about something you left out of your play . . . silence.

CLAUDE:

I know what you're going to say about silence,
Mama . . .

MADELEINE I:

Well, listen anyway. Then, if you quote me again, at
least you'll get it right.   *She places herself very close
to her son.*   You see, in a house like this, it's the
most important thing. It's the only reason the walls
are still standing. Sure, it's true, when your father's
been gone for days and your sister's at work, I get
lonesome. I walk around the house, I don't know
what to do with myself . . . Television is boring and
I've never been a reader . . . I'm past the age when I
have to go out every day, even if it's just for a quart of
milk we don't need . . . So, without fail, I find myself
here, on the sofa, my hands folded on my knees and a
glass of milk on the coffee table in case my pains start
again . . . The first few minutes are always
difficult . . . Every day . . . It's terrifying, my
stomach's in a knot, I don't know how I'm going to
get through the next minute, how I'll survive the
afternoon that's hardly begun . . . Sometimes I'm
paralysed with fear . . . No, that's not right, it's not
fear. I'm not afraid something will happen to me, I
know nothing will happen, nothing! But I'm terrified
because I think I'm going to die from boredom. I've
got nothing to do. If I know your father's not coming
home then I just have a small meal to fix for Mariette
and myself, around six o'clock . . . and if Mariette
calls to say she won't be home, I'm fine with a can of
soup or a sandwich . . .   *Silence. We can sense how
troubled she is.*   So I have . . . five hours to fill. In
silence. And then, in the midst of the silence, the
storm breaks. I feel it coming . . . Sometimes I don't
want it to because I'm too tired or because my side
hurts, but it comes anyway . . . because I need it,
maybe . . . to pass the time. And then . . . it's true
that everything you put in your play goes through my

head . . . I told you earlier they were things I'd never admit to myself . . . Of course, that's not true. I'm not crazy, I know what my life's been like. So, I make up scenes that go on for hours, scenes that are so violent, you can't imagine . . . I throw off my burden, then I take it on again . . . I become . . . some kind of heroine . . . I wreck the house or I burn it down, I slaughter your father, even worse than that . . . I throw fits with you and your sister . . . Everything I wouldn't dare say to you on the phone or when you're here, comes out. It comes out in waves higher than the house. But it all takes place in silence, Claude. If you were to walk in in the middle of it, you'd swear I was daydreaming or just planning tonight's supper . . . because that's the image of myself I always present . . . That's my strength. It's always been that. Silence. I know nothing about theatre, but I'll bet it's tough to do that, a storm in somebody's head! But I'll tell you this much, it's a lot more effective than some domestic brawl. Because it does no harm. I've always put up with things in silence because I know in the long run it pays off. When you barricade yourself in there, you can think whatever you like, even while doing something completely different, and that gives others the impression you want . . . Anyway, what would I gain by doing like you say in your play? If I got a divorce, where would I go? To be bored somewhere else? In some dingy apartment for fools like me who didn't have the sense to shut up? Find myself a job? All I can do is cook and clean house. I'm not about to spend the rest of my days cleaning house for rich people just because once I got things off my chest! And I won't go on having these afternoon nightmares in some two-bit furnished apartment! That woman there in your play, who bears my name and who's dressed like me, what's she going to do the morning after? Eh? After she's played the heroine? You couldn't care less about that! When she opens the door and leaves the stage, she doesn't exist anymore, and you couldn't care less, as long as you've written some wonderful scenes! But me, I have to go on living tomorrow, and the day after

27

tomorrow, and the day after that. If you've never heard the roar of my silence, Claude, you're not a real writer! *Silence.* You've got nothing to say. Admit it, that's not at all what you thought I'd say about silence . . .

CLAUDE:
Yes . . . I admit it. It's true, I didn't see you like that. But I still think your silence is unhealthy. You can't spend a whole lifetime in silence . . .

MADELEINE I:
Yes, you can.

CLAUDE:
A while ago you mentioned your pride . . . You said you were too proud to talk about those things with Papa . . . But your silence, Mama, isn't that humiliating too? It's all very well to sit here and blow off steam in your head, but isn't it humiliating to be an accomplice to everything he's done to you in your life? He's taking a bath, we heard him singing . . . Doesn't his presence insult you? Doesn't his vulgarity, his loud-mouthed, back-slapping grossness, make you shudder? Wouldn't it be more satisfying to go stand over him in his bath and tell him you've known everything all along, that you've nothing but contempt for him?

MADELEINE I:
It's you that needs to do that, Claude. It's your own problems with him you've put in your play, not mine. And I'll tell you something that'll make you shudder. You're unfair to him!

CLAUDE:
Mama!

MADELEINE I:
That's right, unfair!

CLAUDE:
You mean that scene with.

MADELEINE I:
I mean everything! You've made ⌐
someone who's just a poor insignific
insignificant, who tells off-colour joke
fact he's not too bright. He has an unbelie
memory for bad jokes, but it helps him thin.
somebody! That's all. He's not even mean! Su
likes women, he travels and there's every
opportunity . . . but has it ever occured to you that
might suit me? For him to be far away, and have
others?

CLAUDE:
You're not being straight with me, now.

MADELEINE I:
You're right. At this point I'd tell you almost
anything, just to prove you're wrong. *Sharply:*
It's true, I've always swallowed my pride, so what?
That doesn't give you the right to judge me. *She
comes right up to CLAUDE.* I'm all alone inside my
head, Claude, so I'm the only one who knows what I
think. Who are you to speak for me? The Messiah? I'll
save myself, thank you, I don't need you! And I
certainly don't need you to come along and make me
doubt myself! When I read your play, of course I was
shaken. I had doubts. About myself. I doubted I was
right. I saw myself here, in the living room, crucifying
your father, tearing a strip off him with a talent for
smart answers I've never had, and I told myself: what
a beautiful ending, what a splendid way to end it
all. But the consequences terrified me. I'd rather go
on imagining fabulous scenes that I can start and stop
whenever I like, than risk making a permanent mess
of a real one, for which I'd never forgive myself.
Silence. I was so proud of you when you told me
you'd written a play. It's always thrilled me that you
wanted to be a writer . . . I encouraged you all I
could, even when the others teased you . . .

n't tease me, they laughed at me!

ADELEINE I:

Fair enough . . . I said to myself . . . An artist in the
family, a writer especially, that'll be a change . . . I'd
never known anyone who wanted to be an artist. And
all of a sudden there was one in my house! Not so
long ago, when you were still living here, I'd find you
asleep in your bed with a pencil and paper in your
hands . . . You'd come home at night from your
beatnik clubs, you'd grab a piece of paper and shut
yourself up in your room for hours. It frightened me
'cause I thought the people you hung around with
were dangerous . . . but still I was flattered . . . that
here in my house there was someone who was
interested in something other than hockey in winter
and stupid baseball in summer! I'd found an ally to
back me up at eight o'clock on Saturday night.
Remember when you were small, when your father
was home Saturday nights, the arguments we'd have
because we wanted to see the movie on channel 6,
even if it was in English, and your father and Mariette
wanted to watch the hockey game? They'd always
win and you'd slam the door to your room . . . and I
knew what you were doing . . . You didn't ask me to
read what you'd written and I didn't ask you to let
me . . . I waited . . . I guess I waited for what
happened this week . . . for that day when you'd
come and say . . . "Here, read this and tell me what
you think . . . " I was so proud! At last, a big pile of
paper to read . . . I'd never seen a manuscript before.
It didn't look like a book, but there was a chance it
might become one . . . and . . . I was probably one of
the first people to read it . . . before the publisher . . .
before the printer . . . As soon as you left, I came in
here and sat down . . . I was trembling, no kidding! I
told myself . . . at last I'll know . . . what he's been
cooking up all this time . . . I read the title . . . I
wasn't too sure what it meant but that didn't
matter . . . I read the names of the characters . . . I
thought that was sweet of you to give our names to

characters in a play . . . you know . . . I'd never read
a play before and I wasn't too sure how it worked . . .
But . . . after a few pages . . . the deception . . . no,
worse than that . . . I don't know if there's a word to
describe what I felt . . . It was like a burning in my
stomach . . . like the dizziness you feel when you get
some terrible news . . . the betrayal! That's it, I felt
betrayed by my own son . . . I found my whole
life . . . disfigured . . . I could hear Mariette when
you were small, screaming at us that she'd caught you
in the corner again, spying on her . . . and I asked
myself . . . was she right all this time? Have I raised a
spy who copies down everything we say and do so he
can make fools of us later . . . ? Especially
because . . . when all's said and done, you don't
reveal yourself at all. That's what I want to talk to you
about. You talk about everyone in the family but
yourself. Oh, the others mention you, but you're not
there. Never. Why is that? I always thought writers
wrote about themselves . . . to explain
themselves . . . But you, you didn't even have the
courage to put yourself in your own play. By the end
of it, we have no idea who *you* are. You've made us
look horrible in there, you've arranged things to suit
yourself, as you see fit; you've even kept our names,
Claude, but you've hidden yourself. You stand
behind us and you tell the world: look how ugly they
are, how stupid . . .

CLAUDE:
I never said you were ugly or stupid. And if I didn't
talk about myself, it's 'cause I don't think I'm
interesting.

MADELEINE I:
Come off it! You've always done everything around
here to get attention, how come all of a sudden you're
not interesting? I'm more inclined to think it's
cowardice . . . You accuse your father all through the
play of being a coward, but you're no better . . . It's
hardly an act of courage, you know, to write a play
about people who can't defend themselves . . . How

31

are we supposed to answer back? All we can do is sit here, submit to your attacks, put up with your lies, because that's all they are, Claude, lies . . .

CLAUDE:
They're not lies, Mama. It's simply my way of seeing things . . . It's one . . . version of the truth.

MADELEINE I:
Sure, a version you want to present in public while we have to keep our version to ourselves!

CLAUDE:
You say you prefer silence . . . Well, I've decided to speak . . .

MADELEINE I:
But not the truth! You've decided to speak for us, Claude, who gave you that right? And your words are the only ones that'll remain because they're the only ones written down. You've no right to do that! No right! Speak for yourself all you want, talk about yourself, tell us your problems, but leave us alone. I started out thinking I'd finally discover who my son was, but all I found was . . . Ah, I'm not going to repeat it again . . .

CLAUDE:
All writers do that, Mama. They take something they know and they rework it as they see it . . .

MADELEINE I:
That's no excuse! I don't know the other writers and they don't write lies about me. You're just getting in deeper, Claude . . . Is it because you know you can't answer me?

CLAUDE:
Mama . . . you don't know theatre . . .

MADELEINE I:

So why did you have me read it? You hand me a mirror that distorts everything, then you tell me I can't understand it.

CLAUDE:

On the contrary, I told you earlier I thought you'd understand, that you'd appreciate what I tried to do . . .

MADELEINE I:

Appreciate! Appreciate what? Your caricature? Your contempt?

CLAUDE:

Contempt? You really feel contempt in my play? Even for you?

MADELEINE I:

Yes.

CLAUDE:

For Papa, you're right . . . but for you and Mariette . . . I really tried . . . with the best will in the world . . . to defend you . . .

MADELEINE I:

I already told you . . . I don't need you to defend me . . .

CLAUDE:

But what if I needed to defend you? If that was my way of expressing myself? Through the rest of you? Maybe it is spying, and maybe I used everything I thought I knew about you all to say things that aren't pretty to hear . . . that you don't want to hear . . . but I do have the right! And you have to grant me that!

MADELEINE I:

No. No, I don't.

CLAUDE:
> Even if I act in good faith?

MADELEINE I:
> You can't act in good faith. Because you're not us . . .

CLAUDE:
> That's where you're wrong, Mama . . . Listen . . .
> Will you listen to me?   *MADELEINE I sits next to
> CLAUDE.*   It's always been very easy for me . . .
> to slip inside other people. To . . . feel them. I've
> always done that. The rest of you call it spying . . . I
> call it living. When I was in my corner watching you,
> listening to you, I was living intensely everything that
> was going on and everything that was being said. I'd
> record it in my mind, I'd recite it, afterwards I'd add
> things . . . I'd . . . I'd . . . It's true that after I'd
> correct it, what had happened . . . I'd become each
> one of you, I'd slide into each one of you and I'd try to
> understand . . . what it was like inside you . . .
> interpreting, sometimes changing what had
> happened . . . because sometimes what had
> happened wasn't revealing enough . . . That's what I
> still do . . . I try . . . I try to make sense of what goes
> on inside of other people . . .

MADELEINE I:
> And what goes on inside you doesn't interest you?

CLAUDE:
> I told you, I'm not interested in talking about that . . .

MADELEINE I:
> Well, I still say it's cowardice.

CLAUDE:
> Okay, fine . . . I see we can't talk about it . . . we're
> going in circles . . . repeating the same things to no
> end . . . I'm sorry I asked you to read it . . . If you
> like, I'll change the characters' names . . .

MADELEINE I:

What will that change for me? I've read it with my name. I've seen myself suffer in my own living room and say things I'd never say. It's too late! But there's another reason you asked me to read it . . . I know you . . .

CLAUDE:

We're going to put it on in a small theatre next fall, me and my friends.

MADELEINE I:

You're going to take that out of here? You're going to let people read that, perform it, play us? You mean actors are going to be paid to say those things? And people are going to pay to hear them? Don't kid yourself, people won't go to the theatre to see that! They're not crazy! Go on, take it home with you. I don't want to hear another word about it. And if you, you put it on, don't tell me . . . Especially if it's a hit . . .

> *She goes toward the door.*
> *ALEX I comes in in a dressing gown and funny slippers.*
> *MADELEINE I and CLAUDE are clearly ill-at-ease.*

ALEX I:

Jesus Christ, did somebody die around here? Come on, lighten up! I didn't come all this way for a funeral! My God, your chins are on the floor! You know me, when I get home I want a party! You can sort out your problems when I'm not here. How 'bout getting me a nice beer, Madeleine? My throat feels like sandpaper . . . And make it a cold one, the one I had in the bathtub was almost as warm as the water. Yechhh!

> *MADELEINE I goes out silently despite her son's furious expression.*

CLAUDE:
> For God's sake, couldn't you get it yourself?

ALEX I:
> We each have our jobs, my boy. I look after the money, your mother looks after the beer!

CLAUDE:
> How can you say such outrageous things, and find them funny?

ALEX I:
> It's a joke! You know it's a joke. I treat your mother like a queen, and she treats me like the prodigal son! It's been our little game for years, it's none of your concern. Especially you! If anyone's spoiled rotten around here, it's you! *MADELEINE I comes back in with a bottle of beer.* Isn't that right, Mado, you spoil the kids rotten?

MADELEINE I:
> When you start calling me Mado, I know you've got more than one warm beer in your system . . .

CLAUDE:
> See, it's not true you can't answer back . . .

ALEX I:
> Your mother? Answer back? How do you think she hooked me? No one could put a guy in his place like her! She knocked me down to size so often I figured: if I'm gonna take her in hand, I'll have to marry her! But I never succeeded. After twenty-six years of marriage she still has the last word!

MADELEINE I:
> I only get the last word 'cause you start snoring before I finish speaking!

> *She goes out.*

ALEX I: *laughing*
Boy, is it ever good to get home . . . Every time . . .
after all these years . . . How 'bout you, still no
wedding bells?

CLAUDE sighs in exasperation.

ALEX I:
I'm like a broken record, eh? No one gets married
anymore . . . You do your thing together and when it
doesn't work . . . *adios amigos!*   *He drinks.*   I've
been driving so long on bumpy roads, my arms are
still shaking . . . even after a bath . . .

Silence.

Well, I guess I can't count on you for a sparkling
conversation. Were you talking about me when I
came in? I showed up a bit too early, eh? I have the
knack of arriving at the wrong time. Always have! "I
didn't expect you 'til tomorrow," or "I didn't expect
you at all, I thought you were dead!"

CLAUDE:
Must admit, you're not great for giving advance
notice. You show up, we're all supposed to jump!

ALEX I:
You got it, pal! And you're supposed to appreciate
me!   *He laughs.*   You think I'm loud, don't you?
I bet you don't discuss me too often with your beatnik
friends . . .

CLAUDE:
Beatniks went out a long time ago, Papa . . .

ALEX I:
Not that long . . . I can still see you, in your
turtleneck and black pants . . .

CLAUDE:
I was eighteen . . .

ALEX I:

Remember the time I hauled you out of the Paloma
'cause your mother got worried seeing you come
home with bags under your eyes, all strung out from
drinking too much coffee? She even thought you were
on goofballs! Hey, her darling son was hanging out
with a bad crowd . . . getting corrupted! I bet you
were really ashamed of me then, eh? The travelling
salesman father who dares interrupt the sacred
proceedings of the enlightened few who think they're
going to change the world. The stupid, contemptible
working man, who barges in unannounced on the
intellectual elite, the bearers of truth! Remember
what I did when we left? Eh? Bought a round for the
whole gang! I got class!

CLAUDE:

What you don't know is that nobody gave a shit! After
you left they all refused to drink it.

ALEX I gets up, furious.

ALEX I:

You never told me that!

CLAUDE:

I was afraid you'd go smash the place.

ALEX I:

You were right to be afraid, kiddo! Bunch of
screwballs! What a lot of pissy little snobs! Is the
Paloma still open or did some father have the brains
to go burn it down before me?

CLAUDE:

That's you in a nutshell, set fire to anything you don't
understand . . .

ALEX I:

Well, have I got a surprise for you. I'll prove I'm not
as ignorant or as intolerant as you think. Don't look so
stunned, I know the word intolerant. I travel, you

know . . . I'm not like the rest of you . . . I see more than the four walls of a Montreal apartment! I mix with people far more important and interesting than your little gang of nobodies who think they're God's gift to the universe!

CLAUDE:
Oh, I've no doubt you mix with people . . .

ALEX I:
Let me tell you something. I was lying there in my bath with my gut sticking out, my beer in one hand, a washcloth in the other, and I said to myself, I've been unfair to you. That's right. My only son, who I used to be so proud of—'til you went to high school anyway, when you got all your fancy ideas—my only son wants to become a writer and I laugh at him . . . I ought to be proud of him . . . I can just see myself arriving at Thetford Mines or Trois Rivières with your first book . . . I tell you, that'd make a few assholes pucker up with envy . . . Eh? But I said to myself, instead of encouraging him, I put him down before I've read a single line he's written. What if it's good, what if I like it, you never know! We're all alike in this family, eh? Too quick to judge . . . See, you've told me that so often, I start to believe you . . . So, my boy, I decided to ask the big question . . . When you feel like showing me something you've written, any old time, when you're ready, I'm game! How's that grab you? I've decided to give you a fair shake . . . On top of that, I promise I'll read it from start to finish, the whole thing. That's a promise! But I'm warning you, if it's boring you're gonna know about it! What do you say to that? How's that for a father?

CLAUDE:
You'll never be serious, will you? You play the good father, and you're so proud of yourself!

ALEX I:
Not at all, I'm very sincere!

39

ALEX II comes back with the phone.

ALEX II:
What am I gonna do? I can't let them stab me in the
back like that! Nosy bitches, they're all the same,
sooner or later they back you into a corner! Can't hide
a thing from them! Not a goddamn thing. I need a
beer . . . and a good hot bath . . .

He goes toward the kitchen.

ALEX I:
So, what do you say?

CLAUDE: *softly*
You've promised me so many things in my life that
you never gave me . . . I'm sure this is one more
you'll forget . . .

ALEX I:
I never gave you anything?

CLAUDE:
Hold it . . . I didn't say you never gave me
anything . . . I said you'd . . . promised me things . . .

ALEX I:
I always keep my promises. When did I promise you
something I didn't deliver?

CLAUDE:
Papa, my childhood, my adolescence, they're full of
promises you didn't keep . . .

ALEX I:
Oh sure, if you're gonna go back to Genesis . . .

CLAUDE:
That's right, it's in the past, so forget it! How long is
your memory, Papa, two weeks? Three? That's
always been my impression.

ALEX I:
>The important things I remember . . . the rest . . .
>What do you expect, with the life I lead, if I had to
>remember everything . . .

CLAUDE:
>Okay, an example: do you remember the Police
>Youth Association?

ALEX I:
>Police Youth Association? What's that?

CLAUDE:
>You see . . . You went on about that for two years,
>Papa. Two winters in a row you promised to enroll
>me in the Police Youth Association to make a man of
>me, and I believed you. For two years. When you
>came in the door the first thing you'd say was, "Next
>Monday, my boy, put on your white shirt and your
>Sunday pants, we're off to the Police Youth
>Association. They'll make you work out, they'll make
>a man of you, they'll show you what life's all about!
>You'll forget about those books, you'll learn to sweat.
>Buckets!" So every Monday I'd drive Mama crazy 'til
>she got out my best clothes . . . except you were
>never here on Monday. You've never been here
>Mondays, that's probably why you chose that night.
>But I waited for you! Decked out in my best clothes,
>my nose glued to the window . . .

ALEX I:
>I said that to make you happy, Claude, so you'd know
>I was thinking of you, that you were important . . .
>What else could I do, I wasn't around much, I didn't
>want you to forget me . . .

CLAUDE:
>Don't worry, I didn't forget you . . . You were here so
>little I thought of nothing else! It became an
>obsession! And when Mama told us you were on your
>way home, I'd get so excited I'd have a fever! Every
>time, every time I'd wait for an explanation . . . I'd

41

have believed any lie, no matter how big, rather than admit to myself it was an empty promise . . . You'd walk in, you'd make your same friggin' promise, and you'd go take your friggin' bath! And I believed you! And I kept telling my friends: next Monday my father's taking me to the Police Youth Association, and they're going to teach me to kick the shit out of you! Of course they'd all laugh at me, but I didn't care! Each time I was sure this was it! And the following week we'd start again. You'd get out of your bath, put on your friggin' dressing gown, and not a word about the Police Youth Association. I followed you like a puppy, my heart racing, I couldn't take my eyes off you, I was practically in your lap while you were eating . . . You, you'd make your promise, you weren't even aware of me . . .

ALEX I:
Come on, don't try to tell me I ruined your life 'cause I didn't enroll you in the Police Youth Association . . .

CLAUDE:
When you pretend not to understand like that, it's so insulting . . . I give you an example, just one. Ah, forget it!

ALEX I:
Why do you bring this up all of a sudden?

CLAUDE:
Because what I write is directly related to it . . . so maybe you should read it . . .

ALEX I:
You talk about me in the stuff you write?

MADELEINE II comes in rubbing her wrist, followed by ALEX II.

ALEX II:
You worry about what goes on in the house, don't stick your nose in what happens elsewhere!

MADELEINE II:
>I didn't have to! What happened elsewhere came to me!

ALEX II:
>Don't talk back! I know you can answer back! Always thought you were smarter than me, eh? I know you! You watch every move I make, judge everything I say, but you don't mind taking the money I bring home, do you? Well I'm telling you, you're staying here! I didn't sweat blood raising a family to find myself twenty-five years later with a wife and kids who despise me! Or alone after a humiliating divorce!

ALEX I:
>You watch your step, my boy! You watch what you say about me! I've been patient with you, I've let a lot of things go by, but my patience has a limit! I haven't sacrificed all my life to support you and the others to find myself with a thankless kid who stabs me in the back first chance he gets! You've always looked down on me, always thought you were smarter than me, but you watch your step! If you push me far enough, and all I've got left are my fists, you'll really be sorry I didn't take you to the Police Youth Association!

ALEX II:
>It's the first time I've touched you in twenty-five years, but if that's what it takes . . .

MADELEINE II:
>It is not the first time you've touched me . . . You've got a short memory!

CLAUDE:
>You've used your fists already, don't you remember?

THE TWO ALEXES:
>That's not true . . .

ALEX II:
>I've never touched you . . .

ALEX I:
> I've never laid a hand on any of you . . .

CLAUDE:
> That's true, you're right . . . you threatened to once,
> but you didn't . . .

ALEX I:
> I threatened to more than once, and maybe I should
> have more than once. Maybe I'd get a little more
> respect around here!

ALEX II:
> When? When did I touch you?

ALEX I:
> If you're gonna start inventing things! You can hold it
> against me for the promises I made and didn't keep
> when you were small 'cause I didn't know how else
> to get you off my back, but don't make up things that
> might have consequences! I never hit you, never, so
> don't let me hear you say otherwise!

MADELEINE II:
> If you've managed to forget, good for you. It was the
> best thing you could do, I suppose . . .

ALEX II:
> I didn't manage to forget, I don't remember!

MADELEINE II:
> I'm not surprised. That's you in a nutshell. What you
> don't like, you don't see . . . or you just forget.
> Nevertheless . . . it was a horrible moment in my
> life . . .

ALEX II:
> Okay, it was a horrible moment. Christ, at this rate
> we'll have to canonize you before the night's out!

MADELEINE II:
Alex, please, don't make jokes. It won't work, not
today.

CLAUDE:
Papa, may I ask you a question?

ALEX I:
I don't know. To be honest, I don't know what to
expect from you now.

ALEX II:
Okay . . . look . . . what did I do that was so
terrible? . . . When? . . . I honestly think if I ever
raised a hand to you, I'd remember . . .

MADELEINE II:
Once, only once in my life, I asked you to look after
the kids . . .

ALEX II starts.

CLAUDE:
Remember once, when we were small, Mariette and
I, Mama asked you to look after us . . .

ALEX I:
Do I remember! Yeah, I was so bored I got plastered!
'Specially since Mariette was at least twelve or
thirteen, and was old enough to babysit . . . See, I told
you your mother was over-protective . . .

He goes out to the kitchen.

MADELEINE II:
Mother was dying, and the family decided we should
all be with her . . .

ALEX II:
Don't start on that! I told you, I never want to hear
about that night again!

45

MADELEINE II:

Because you don't want to talk about it doesn't mean it didn't happen, Alex . . .

ALEX II:

It didn't happen, goddamnit! It was all in your head! That's what always scared me. I saw something in your eyes that night I'd never seen before and . . . You're right, I decided to forget it! Okay, I admit I'd forgotten some of it! But I don't want to talk about it now any more than I did then . . .

MADELEINE II:

I also saw things in your eyes that night, Alex, things I'd never seen before! But I could never forget them, even if I spent the rest of my life trying!

ALEX II:

If you ask me, you've made a point of not forgetting! 'Specially since nothing happened that night, and you know it!

He grabs her by the wrist.

ALEX II:

If something had really happened that night, you'd have taken the kids and left. Your accusations were so horrible, you'd never have wanted to see me again! The proof that nothing happened is that you stayed!

MADELEINE II:

I stayed because I had no place to go . . .

ALEX II:

You stayed because you knew you'd imagined it! It's true I hit you that night, I remember very well . . . Yeah, I smacked you one, and you know what? You deserved it! You drag it up again tonight 'cause you think you're gonna dump me, and it suits you to keep finding reasons to do it! I'm not blind, you know . . . You're a goddamn hypocrite and you know it!

Silence.
MADELEINE II goes up to her husband and looks him straight in the eye.

MADELEINE II:
Mariette told me everything that night. A child of thirteen doesn't lie about those things! If you don't want to discuss it, that's fine. I think I'd prefer it that way myself. But I want you to know once and for all that I've always known, and if I never said anything it's because I was afraid. A man who can do things like that is capable of anything . . .

ALEX I returns with his beer.

CLAUDE:
You remember what happened that night?

ALEX I sits in an armchair.

MADELEINE II:
Have you ever felt you've been buried under a ton of bricks? Or hit over the head with a hammer? Because in a split second your whole life got changed? One moment, you're someone with a certain frame of mind . . . you're sure you know who you are and who the others are around you . . . You don't question anything about them . . . haven't for ages. Your world . . . is definitive. My world was definitive, Alex. I had . . . arrived somewhere . . . for good. I understood everything that had happened to me. I even had . . . a grip on my most serious problems . . . which weren't really all that bad, but could have kept me from being happy if I hadn't had them in hand . . . Mother's death shook me up, that's certain, but we'd all expected it and I knew I'd get over it . . . That evening, I came home from her place . . . at peace with myself. I'd done my duty, mother had talked to me, I'd managed to calm her down a bit, she was so scared of dying . . . It's hard to explain . . . When I climbed the stairs I was someone very precise . . . and when I opened the door I became someone

47

else . . . At that exact moment I was forced to become someone else . . . because all of a sudden my whole life collapsed around me. It was as if I'd entered into someone else's skin . . . and it wasn't even someone I wanted to know. With no warning I was forced to jump from one life to another. My husband, my children, had changed while I was away. I'd left a perfectly happy and quiet household and all of a sudden I landed back in some kind of . . . incomprehensible hell. When you hit me, I didn't even feel it. It wasn't me you hit, it was the other one . . . the unhappy woman I still didn't know . . . I couldn't even hate you right away, I had so little notion of what was happening . . . *She looks at ALEX II.* But since then I've had time to catch up, though I've never been able to tell you . . . rather I've let the chances go by . . . out of . . . fear probably . . . Ever since then I've been afraid of you, Alex . . . But today it's my turn to make you change your world. When you came through that door a while ago, you entered another world. How does it feel? *ALEX II doesn't answer. MADELEINE II shrugs her shoulders and goes out.*

ALEX I:
Nothing happened. I watched the hockey game, you whined all night 'cause you couldn't stand it, and Mariette sulked 'cause I wouldn't let her go out . . . Why do you want to know? You're not still on about whether or not I hit you? I no more hit anyone that night than any other!

MARIETTE I bursts in.

MARIETTE I:
My favourite Papa!

ALEX I:
My favourite daughter!

*They throw themselves in each other's arms.
CLAUDE is ill-at-ease.*

48

ALEX I:
> You're just in time! Your brother's giving me the third degree about something that happened before the flood!

MARIETTE I:
> That's how he gets his kicks these days . . . Hi, little brother . . . Still picking at old wounds? The last six weeks, he hasn't let me alone either . . . He's got an incredible memory, you know. He's been telling me stuff I'd forgotten since I was a kid!

ALEX I:
> Yeah, and if you ask me, he's getting dangerous.

> > *MARIETTE II comes in, closing her umbrella. She sees her father on the sofa.*
> > *She leans against the door frame.*

MARIETTE II:
> Are you examining your conscience?

> > *ALEX II jumps.*

ALEX II:
> You scared me . . .

> > *She comes into the living room, removing her raincoat.*

ALEX I:
> How're ya doin', Baby-doll?

MARIETTE I:
> A-one! Bone tired, 'cause I've been working too hard, but, you know, when you're tired like that, it makes you feel good . . .

ALEX I:
> Still kicking up your heels?

MARIETTE I:
> It's all I know how to do! That and things you don't
> tell your papa . . .

> *They laugh.*

MARIETTE II:
> Mama was pretty worried . . . you should phone
> when you know you're gonna be a few days late . . .

ALEX II:
> I don't know when I'm gonna be late . . .

MARIETTE II:
> Doesn't cost much to phone . . .

ALEX II:
> Sometimes I don't want to listen to her
> complaints . . . Calling here is like punching the
> clock! I chose a line of work where I'd be free to move
> around 'cause I didn't want to be cooped up in a
> factory all my life. Your mother knows that, I've told
> her a thousand times . . . I like my freedom!

ALEX I:
> I saw you on T.V. the other night . . . Thanks for
> calling to let me know . . . I tell you, that made 'em
> drool . . . Hey, my daughter on T.V . . . They
> couldn't believe it . . . neither could I . . . We got a
> good shot of you, too . . . Not for long, but we
> recognized you . . . Too bad colour T.V. isn't here yet.

MARIETTE I:
> Looks like I'll be on even more next time . . . Hey,
> did you know I was one of the first gogo dancers in
> Montreal? . . . I got experience! I show the others
> how to do it . . .

ALEX I:
> You sure know how to shake it. You should have seen
> the guys at Hotel Lapointe . . .

MARIETTE I:

You should see the studio technicians! Boy, do we
have fun . . . You know, if this keeps up I won't have
to dance in the clubs all the time . . .

MARIETTE II:

Speaking of freedom . . . was that a coincidence the
other night?

ALEX II:

The other night . . .

MARIETTE II:

Papa, don't play dumb! The other night, the Hotel
Rancourt in Victoriaville!

ALEX II:

Oh, yeah . . . yeah, that was a coincidence . . .

ALEX I:

You can make your living on television?

MARIETTE I:

No, but with television I can slack off a bit . . . It's not
easy, you know, climbing into that cage every night
and wiggling your ass for hours . . . It's not
something casual I do to relax . . . It's work, I do it
every night! Hardly ever in the same place! Some of
the dumps I see . . . you wouldn't believe me if I told
you . . .

ALEX I:

Mariette . . . I travel too, you know!

MARIETTE I:

Yeah, I guess you see some doozers too . . . But you
never talk about them . . . You never tell us your
adventures on the highroads of Quebec . . . I have a
sneaking suspicion that some of them aren't too
tellable . . . you're such a rascal . . .

ALEX II:
> I didn't even know you were in the area . . . I just
> happened to go in . . .

MARIETTE II:
> And you just happened to be with six of your
> salesman friends . . .

ALEX II:
> Mariette . . . Saturday nights, we often get together
> for a drink . . .

MARIETTE I:
> I bet Claude would love to hear them . . . wouldn't
> you, Claude? Boy, the questions you'd ask Mama to
> find out what Papa does on his weekends . . .

ALEX II:
> We all know where to find each other. We leave
> messages . . .

CLAUDE:
> Didn't you want to know?

MARIETTE I:
> Sure, but I didn't bug Mama about it . . .

MARIETTE II:
> And once a month you just happen to stumble on a
> hotel where I'm working!

CLAUDE:
> No, knowing you, you'd go directly to him . . .

MARIETTE I:
> Look who's jealous . . .

CLAUDE:
> I'm not jealous!

ALEX I:
> Leave him be, he's in a bad mood today . . . Don't
> bother him, he bites!

> *They laugh.*

MARIETTE II:
> Look, while we're alone . . . there's something I want
> to ask you . . . It's embarrassing, Papa, to dance on a
> stage when you know you're father's watching . . .

ALEX II:
> For Chrissake, you're not doing a striptease!

MARIETTE II:
> You shout louder than the others, you clap louder . . .
> You and your buddies aren't too subtle, Papa . . . I
> don't know . . . it's unhealthy . . .

ALEX II:
> Unhealthy! What's unhealthy?

MARIETTE II:
> Papa, it's as if you're selling me! There you are,
> following me around month after month with a
> bunch of drunks . . . The hotel managers have started
> calling you my fan club . . . Good thing they don't
> know you're my father! Put yourself in my place!
> There I am busting my ass on stage to get people to
> dance and drink, and I know my own father's out
> there making jokes with a bunch of pigs who think
> I'm just a piece of meat!

ALEX II:
> If you can't handle it, find another job!

MARIETTE II:
> I can handle it! I've been doing it long enough! But
> not in front of my father! Can't you understand?

MARIETTE I:
Ah, well . . . Before he was just jealous, now he's
ashamed too . . .

CLAUDE:
Great . . . here we go . . .

MARIETTE I:
I'll bet you weren't glued to the T.V. the other night
when your gogo girl sister made her debut!

CLAUDE:
No, you're right, but that doesn't mean I'm
ashamed . . . That kind of show doesn't interest me,
that's all . . . And I sure wouldn't watch it just 'cause
my sister's making a fool of herself locked up in some
cage, dancing like a monkey in a mini-skirt!

MARIETTE II:
I can see your eyes, you know . . . Yours as much as
the others'!

CLAUDE:
Sorry. I sound like a shit, I don't mean that . . .

MARIETTE I:
Oh, yes you do . . .

ALEX II:
What's wrong with my eyes . . .

MARIETTE II:
They're ugly! Like the others'!

MARIETTE I:
You and your snooty airs, you can't fool me . . .
You've always spied on me, you've always twisted
everything I said and did. When you were a kid you
were always snooping around, minding other
peoples' business. We never knew where you were.
You were always creeping around behind some
armchair or hiding in a closet . . . You spent your

childhood spying on us! You wouldn't say a word for days, but we knew you'd listened to everything we'd said. *She sighs in exasperation.* Ah, why am I saying all this? I was in a good mood when I came in . . .

ALEX I:
> 'Course you were, now relax . . . How 'bout a beer with your old man . . . We haven't seen each other for weeks . . .

MARIETTE I:
> You know he came all the way up to Shawinigan to ask me questions . . . I don't know what stage he's going through, but boy, is he weird . . . He wanted to know what happened one night when you babysat us, when Grandma was dying . . . Can you remember that?

ALEX I:
> Jesus-Christ, he's got a one-track mind! You bet I remember, I'd never babysat before and I thought I'd go nuts . . . You were a giant pain, the pair of you . . . You, you wouldn't go to sleep unless I sat beside your bed and held your hand . . . You sulked for hours when I wouldn't let you go out, then you wouldn't let me leave you alone . . . I think I fell asleep too . . . Too much beer . . .

CLAUDE:
> Yeah, that's always been your version . . .

MARIETTE II:
> Look, I'm not accusing you . . . but when you've had lots to drink and heard lots of jokes about me . . . don't you forget sometimes I'm your daughter?

ALEX II:
> What do you mean?

MARIETTE II:
> Well, you did forget once . . .

CLAUDE:
> And we all chose to believe it . . .

> *ALEX I laughs.*

ALEX I:
> Claude, I can't believe you would think . . .

MARIETTE I:
> You must be sick!

ALEX II:
> Okay, so I forgot once! Okay!

MARIETTE I:
> You're sick in the head!

ALEX II:
> But it was no big deal . . . I stopped in time . . .

MARIETTE II:
> That's not true! If Claude hadn't come in . . .

ALEX I:
> Jesus-Christ! All this time you've been thinking that of me!

CLAUDE:
> You'd been playing around with each other, for some time . . .

MARIETTE II:
> You'd been playing around with me for some time . . . 'Course we'd always done that . . .

MARIETTE I:
> Maybe so, but Claude, we always did that . . . Papa played with you too! He did that with everyone . . . I'm sure he still does it, even if it's not with us anymore . . . He's a touchy-feely guy, that's all! It's not a disease!

MARIETTE II:
Of course it was nice when I was a kid . . . My father
was different from the others . . . He wasn't just
funny, he was loveable! We were always kissing and
holding hands . . . You'd sweet-talk me so much I'd
get goose-bumps . . . I'd kiss you on the ear and you'd
tell me you could feel it to the tips of your toes . . .

MARIETTE I:
It's true, for a while there it bothered me, but . . .

MARIETTE II:
Naturally I liked it . . . You were like Santa Claus . . .
We hardly ever saw you, so when you came home
you were . . . superimportant. Everything was
different, nothing else counted . . . you were the
centre of everything . . .

MARIETTE I:
Do you remember when I started to fill out . . . I was
so embarrassed, I tried to hide it but they wouldn't go
away . . . You, when you came home that time, you
wouldn't let up! I was so ashamed! You pulled out all
your farmer's daughter jokes, I thought I'd die! I even
asked Mama to buy me an old lady's nightgown, and I
wore it around the house hoping nothing would
show . . . Talk about naive! One thing's for sure, I
didn't let you play with me then . . . nor the next
time . . . No more horsing around, eh! I left that to
Claude, who kept himself quite busy, if I
remember . . . Anyway, I was so embarrassed by the
changes that were happening in me, I could hardly
look you guys in the face . . .

She laughs.

MARIETTE I:
I could talk about it with my friends, that was
easy . . . but with you . . . and even with Mama, it
was impossible . . . I was a big girl, and that was
it . . . Oh, she'd explained it, all the physical stuff . . .
but it made no difference! Now, when I think back on

that time . . . I miss it . . . even if I was miserable . . . It's nice to think those things made me blush . . . I miss being dumb and naive . . . sometimes I wish I still were.

MARIETTE II:

But it wasn't so nice when I became a woman . . . I changed . . . and so did you. You didn't look at me the same way any more . . . Oh, you were still funny, still a Santa Claus, but there was something new that made me uneasy . . . I'd catch you staring at me without saying anything . . . It gave me the creeps . . . Your kisses . . . were more insistent . . . your jokes more pointed . . . your compliments more embarrassing. Mama began telling you not to play with me so much . . . I wasn't sure why, but something told me she was right. So you horsed around with Claude, halfheartedly. You never paid him much attention, did you? Sometimes we thought it was because you weren't interested in the same things . . . You even laughed at him, at his books and T.V. shows you thought were stupid . . . Anyway, you were still buzzing around me without . . . getting too close . . . until that night . . .

ALEX II:

Don't talk about that. It's a dead issue, I've sorted it out.

MARIETTE II:

You've sorted it out, that's all that counts! What happened to me doesn't matter!

MARIETTE I:

You know what? When you came and lay down beside me that night, everything felt right again . . . I had my old papa, and that made me feel good. Santa was back.

ALEX I: *to CLAUDE*
You see?

MARIETTE I:
That was the last time in my life I felt like a little girl.
It was sort of a turning point. I fell asleep too, I
think . . . like you . . . But then snoopy here turned
up! The cries, the tears, the drama . . . Poor Mama
comes running in, she doesn't know what's
happened . . . we must have woken the whole bloody
neighbourhood! I was hysterical, I was bawling like a
baby . . . and the whole thing ended in a horrible
misunderstanding . . .   *to Claude*   Thanks to
you . . .

MARIETTE II:
Your smell of beer, your crazy eyes . . . Not much
like Santa, that's for sure! Can you imagine what it's
like for a young girl to see her father in that state? I
tried to tell myself you'd been drinking, you were
angry at me 'cause I'd been bad, you didn't know
what you were doing . . . There are no explanations,
Papa, no excuses! That cuts a life in two! It breaks . . .
something for ever! It destroyed everything I felt for
you . . . all the admiration . . . the love. Just like that.
In that one night, I grew older. And you . . . you died.
Then Claude came in, just in time, and all hell broke
loose . . . He was probably jealous, but never
mind . . . it saved me . . . literally . . . Because if he
hadn't come in . . . and if Mama hadn't arrived and
stood up for us . . . We both saw you hit her, Papa,
because she knew what was going to happen! You hit
her because you were about to do something
monstrous! Instead of punishing yourself, you
punished her! Someone else always pays, don't they!
You can't face yourself, so you punish others!   *She
comes very close to her father.*   And I relive the
whole thing when you come to see me dance! That's
exactly how I feel! I can see you, you know. The stage
isn't so bright I can't see you, you and your friends!
And the way you look at me, there's no difference
between you and them. None! How do explain it to
them, what you're doing, how can you look them in
the face? Or is that part of the trip? Does it turn them
on, knowing you're gonna watch your own daughter

59

dance in every sleazy hotel in the province? You can't answer. You really don't want to talk about it, do you?

MARIETTE I: *to CLAUDE*
Is that clear enough for you? Does it satisfy your sick curiosity? What you thought was monstrous was nothing at all . . .

ALEX II:
I've had to live with that . . . ever since, Mariette! You understand . . . if I have to talk about it too . . .

MARIETTE II:
It might do you good.

ALEX II:
To forget will do me good. Nothing more. Nothing less.

MARIETTE II:
Fine, so forget me! I came to ask you . . . no, not to ask . . . I came to tell you, never come to see me dance again, Papa! You hear? If you ever set foot in a club where I'm dancing, I'll do something you'll never forget! After that, those pigs you call friends won't give you the time of day! You'll be branded for life! I'm through being humiliated by you when I'm trying to work, now it'll be your turn!   *She picks up her umbrella and raincoat.*   Tell Mama I came by to pick up my umbrella and couldn't stay 'cause my taxi was waiting . . .

She leaves.

ALEX II:
I don't take orders from you! My Saturday nights are mine and I'll do what I fucking please! Neither of you broads will change a thing in my life, okay!

He finishes his beer.

ALEX I: *to CLAUDE*

I see now, I should have given you the thrashing you
deserved that night . . . Might have knocked some
sense into you. Instead of making up lies, inventing
stories, why didn't you come and see me? You prefer
your own version, eh? Is that it? It's more exciting to
imagine something happened! And then drag it
around for years! Well, if that's your image of me,
kiddo . . .

CLAUDE:

It's always the same around here. If anything serious
happens, it ends up having no importance because
you all prefer it that way! How many laundered
versions of things have I heard? I know I can't win
against you . . . maybe that's why I do something else
with what happened here . . .

MARIETTE I:

You still think you're right?

CLAUDE:

I don't know if I'm right. I'm searching . . .

ALEX I:

Don't search too hard! Things may be a lot simpler
than what's in your head . . .

CLAUDE:

Maybe they're more complicated than you'd care to
admit!

ALEX II:

Why is everything so complicated?

MARIETTE I approaches her brother.

MARIETTE I:
>Complicate your life all you want, but leave us out of it. All of us. Okay? Do your snooping elsewhere, maybe it'll smell worse, the way you like it . . . Here . . . it just smells normal . . . That's not interesting . . . We're not interesting enough for you, Claude . . . We're not sick enough . . .

>*She leaves.*

ALEX II:
>It was so simple the way it was. So simple. When I was small, my mother always said: "You can never get home scott free." I thought she was crazy. And all my life I've tried to prove her wrong. I've busted my ass to hang on to my freedom, and I'll be damned if I'm gonna lose it! Why should I pay now for stuff that happened ages ago? I'm not gonna pay! I won't! They'll take me as I am, like it or lump it! Who's boss around here, eh? I'm not gonna be led around by the nose! Not by some hysterical cow who doesn't know what she's saying, nor by some gogo dancer who doesn't want people to see her dance! I'll see her dance all I want. If she wants to show off her tits, let her show 'em! It's good for business. My pals envy me, so do my clients! And when I watch her, I'll think what I like!

>*He drinks.*

ALEX II:
>You bring up a kid . . . a little doll you can play with all you want . . . You can kiss her on her bum, her tummy, kiss her little mouth, tickle her . . . For years you can do what you like with her, it's just a game, just for fun, it's daddy and his little girl having fun . . . You see her growing up, sometimes so fast it worries you, but no big deal, she's still your baby girl and you go on tossing her in the air, pretending you won't catch her, to give her a scare so she'll hug you a little harder . . . Then one day . . . the conspiracy begins . . . the conspiracy of women . . . It starts with

whispers in the hallway . . . You think they're talking behind your back . . . hiding something from you . . . something you should know, but they don't want to tell you . . . and your little girl's not as cuddly either . . . suddenly she's modest . . . blushes more easily . . . You want to keep playing, but your baby, who's changing before your very eyes, hesitates, runs away, she finds excuses for not coming too close . . . Christ, it's almost like being jilted! You think she's turned her back on you because you've done something, and you don't know what! Then one day you manage to get her on the sofa . . . You were so happy, it was the first time in ages! After a few cuddles, just like the old days, you feel . . . you too, for the first time . . . you feel that something's changed . . . Not just in her eyes . . . Her body . . . Beneath her blouse . . . And it all comes clear. The conspiracy! If she's afraid of you, it's got to be her mother who's told her that now she's a big girl she mustn't touch her father any more! So it's them! It's the women. They put those ideas in your head! You just wanted your child to stay a child, but they put something else in your head, that if you feel like it . . . Well, I felt like it! It's too bad, but I felt like it! And . . . I still do!

He finishes his beer.

I'm thirsty . . . I'm thirsty! I want a beer! I want someone to get me a beer! It's my house, I paid for it, I paid for everything, it's all mine, and I want a beer!

MADELEINE I comes in.

MADELEINE I:
Dinner's served. Come and sit down. But I want to talk to Claude first.   *to ALEX I*   Go sit down, Mariette's already there . . . I'll be right in.

He goes out.

63

ALEX II:
I want a beer!

> *MADELEINE I jumps.*
> *Silence.*
> *MADELEINE II enters the room.*
> *She is holding ALEX II's suitcase in one hand, and a*
> *beer in the other.*

MADELEINE II:
Here! Here's your beer. But it's your last. And the
pleasure's all mine.

ALEX II:
What do you mean, my last?

MADELEINE II:
Don't play dumb. No point your staying here tonight,
eh? Things might get out of hand. The mere thought
of you in this house kills me, Alex.

> *MADELEINE I takes CLAUDE's manuscript and*
> *hands it to him.*

MADELEINE I:
I don't want you to stay for supper tonight . . . I'm
not throwing you out, I'm just asking you not to
stay . . . I'd feel you were spying on us again, I
wouldn't be able to talk, I'd be anxious about
everything your father said . . . I don't think I can
ever be natural again with you, Claude . . . *She
goes towards the kitchen door.* And don't call. Wait
to hear from me.

> *She leaves.*

ALEX II:
You think you can toss me out?

MADELEINE II:
You bet I do. I've had it! I've put up with enough,
swallowed enough, I'm through tearing myself to
pieces . . . I'm tired of telling myself I'm wrong about
you, that deep down you're a good guy who's just not
too bright and not very responsible . . . I'm fed up.
I've had enough. If you don't leave, I will . . .

ALEX II:
You're not leaving. And neither am I. Things will stay
as they are, okay!

MADELEINE II:
Be careful, Alex. I've always been gentle and
understanding, but there's a whole other side of me
you don't know. Everyone has a hidden side, you're
not the only one who can fool people. So watch out
for what you don't know about me.

ALEX II:
Threats?

MADELEINE II:
I suppose you could call it that. It makes me feel good
to know I can threaten you, Alex! I see a flicker of
doubt in your eyes, and I like it . . . I think you're
really getting scared . . . Your view of things is
changing, eh? It's not as clear as it was . . . Well, what
you see now is nothing compared with what you'd
see if I let myself go! I've got twenty-five years of
frustration inside me, Alex, and I hope for your sake
it doesn't all come out at once. Believe me, you'd be a
lot smarter to find a hotel tonight . . . It'll save
you . . . a lot of cruel words, some unpleasant
surprises, and some devastating insults. But if you
prefer, if you insist, if you choose to stay, I'm ready to
face you, tell you everything. Everything. I can do
amazing things tonight, Alex; I can also save you from
them. I'll give you time to choose . . . time enough for
a beer which, in any case, is your last. When I come
back, if you're still here, watch out.

We hear the third movement of Mendelsohn's fifth symphony. MADELEINE II slowly goes up to CLAUDE and taps him on the shoulder as if to say "good work."
She in turn goes out.
CLAUDE and ALEX II are alone on stage.
ALEX II puts his head in his hands.
CLAUDE hugs his manuscript.

ALEX II: *straightening up*
If there's nothing left for me, there'll be nothing for you either.

Very deliberately, he trashes the living room. He leaves.

ALEX I enters slowly, goes up to CLAUDE and takes the manuscript out of his hands.

ALEX I:
Is this the only one, or are there copies?

CLAUDE:
It's my only one.

ALEX II:
That's risky.

CLAUDE:
I know. But I haven't had time. One of my friends said she'd give me stencils . . . I've got other things to do, you know. I've got a job, I have to earn a living too . . . I wrote this at work, in my spare time; on the corner of my boss's desk when he wasn't there; at home, nights, instead of going out . . . weekends . . .

ALEX I:
I see, a hobby . . .

CLAUDE: *sharply*
It's a lot more than a hobby, and you know it!

ALEX I:
> No, I don't know. I don't know much of anything about you . . .

> *He leafs through the manuscript.*

CLAUDE:
> There's not much about me that's ever interested you . . .

ALEX I:
> You're repeating yourself . . .

CLAUDE:
> Not enough, maybe . . .

ALEX I:
> So if I tore it up right now, if I set fire to it, it would disappear completely . . . It wouldn't exist anymore . . .

> *CLAUDE looks at him for a few seconds.*

CLAUDE:
> Are you trying to frighten me?

ALEX I:
> Yep. If I were you I'd be afraid. A crazy father who doesn't want his kid to talk about him in his "works" . . .

CLAUDE:
> As long as you're making fun of me, I know you won't do anything . . .

> *ALEX II throws the manuscript in the air. The pages fly all over the room. CLAUDE doesn't react.*

ALEX I:
> Now are you scared?

CLAUDE:
No.

ALEX I picks up a page at random.

ALEX I:
"Alex: What am I gonna do? I can't let them stab me in the back like that . . . Nosy bitches, they're all the same, sooner or later they back you into a corner!" What am I talking about? Your mother and sister? Or women in general?

He crumples up the page, tosses it across the room.

ALEX I:
Anyway, you've no right to use my name.

CLAUDE:
I already talked to Mama about that . . . I'm changing the names . . .

ALEX I:
There's the problem . . . You've always talked to your mother . . .

CLAUDE:
You were never here . . .

ALEX I:
Don't give me that Police Youth Association crap! You and your mother have been carrying on behind my back over more important things than that.

He comes over to CLAUDE and sits down beside him on the sofa.

ALEX I:
Come on, shoot. Now's the time. Let's hear everything you've got against me, I'm all ears. Unless of course you've worked it all out with your mother . . . I was too polite to listen to what you were saying earlier, but maybe I should have. Now there's

a fault I don't have: I don't eavesdrop! That must disappoint you! Come on, I don't feel like reading your great literature anymore, it might make me sick, so tell it to me, we'll have a good laugh . . .

CLAUDE:
You've always been good at defusing an important conversation . . . How do you expect us to talk seriously . . . You're already making light of everything we might say . . .

> *ALEX I almost jumps on his son, grabbing him by the collar.*

ALEX I:
I take none of this lightly, okay?

> *They look at each other a few seconds.*
> *ALEX I moves away from CLAUDE.*

ALEX I:
You like that better? The brute instead of the joker? Isn't that how you've always seen me? . . . You think I have to read that to know what you think of me? Come off it! If you needed therapy so bad, instead of tearing your heart out writing bullshit about me, why didn't you come and see me on one of my rounds? One weekend in a hotel room in Saint-Jérôme, we could have straightened this out . . . a long time ago, too . . .

CLAUDE:
That's where you're wrong . . . All you'd have straightened out is your side of things! As usual. You'd have put on a non-stop show for two days, a clever but endless monologue, mildly amusing and totally egocentric . . . You wouldn't have known I was there . . . Are you ever aware of other people when you talk? Do you ever answer their questions, wait for their answers? It's not conversations you have, it's spectacular monologues! Are you all the same, you and your buddies? Do you talk in

monologues instead of listening to each other? When you're together in Saint-Jérôme, for instance, do you all talk at the same time?

ALEX I:

Where do you get this crap? . . . You never came to Saint-Jérôme, you never wanted to. How can you guess, much less judge, what goes on there?

CLAUDE picks up several pages and waves them under his father's nose.

CLAUDE:

Do you know how long I've worked on this? How many years? With my imagination, that's right, with what I could guess about you? Do you know it's because of you I began to write? And because you always acted as if you were deaf? The first time I put a pencil to paper, I was eleven, maybe twelve, it was to talk to you 'cause I couldn't reach you, it was to tell you I loved you 'cause you probably would have slugged me if I'd actually said it . . . There were so many things we couldn't talk about in this house, I had to put them on paper or suffocate! It was my only outlet, and it gave me as much release as when I first started to masturbate! And writing made me feel just as guilty afterwards because it seemed even more forbidden! "Speaking to one's father is absolutely forbidden under pain of mortal sin, irremediable and irrevocable!" I struggled for hours trying to paint an idyllic picture of you, I described you as I wanted you to be . . . here! Just as funny, just as lively, but HERE! I didn't tear my heart out, not at all, on the contrary . . . I was so exhilarated by what I wrote, I'd nearly faint! I discovered the exhilaration of writing by making declarations of love to my father who didn't want to know about me!

ALEX I:

Shit, I left my smokes in the kitchen . . .

70

CLAUDE:
See , you don't want to listen! Even though you asked!

ALEX I:
You're starting again, just like when you were a
kid . . . you're starting again! Clinging, saying things
nobody wants to hear!

CLAUDE:
What things? What things? Name them. Come on, see
if you can name them!

ALEX I:
Feelings! Feelings! I always ran away from you; I fled,
'cause it always comes back to that!

CLAUDE:
Why shouldn't it come back to that? What prevented
us? Was there some rule, some law?   *ALEX I starts*
to get up.   Don't run away. For once, please, don't
run away . . .

ALEX I:
It's the way I am, that's all . . . I've never talked
about my feelings . . . to anyone . . . and I'm not
gonna start now.   *He looks his son in the eye.*
Surely you could have guessed, behind the clown
routines, the travelling salesman jokes . . . surely you
could have guessed that behind all that there were
feelings! Because I don't talk about them doesn't
mean they're not there! If they don't want to come
out, they won't. Don't make it a tragedy!

CLAUDE:
A child can't live on guesses! Or silence! We were
often on the verge of saying things, Papa, but it never
happened! We horsed around a lot, oh, did we ever,
tickling each other, charging all over the house,
exhausting ourselves playing hide and seek, but when
we were all out of breath and we'd look each other in
the eye like we are now, when something truly
important might have happened between us . . .

ALEX I:
I can't, that's all! I can't! Don't ask me anymore!

CLAUDE:
Don't worry, I won't. I don't ask you for anything now. *He picks up a page.* I'm just telling you why "this" exists. When you can't talk, things have to come out some other way.

ALEX I:
Fine, now we've got something important. Let's talk about how it came out. You say when you were small, you had this idyllic picture of me. Something tells me that "this," as you say, is none too idyllic! Your image of me has changed in ten years, eh? Something tells me there's not much left of "Papa, I love you, my wonderful papa!"

CLAUDE:
Believe it or not, understanding comes with age.

ALEX I:
Understanding! Of what? I didn't become a monster between 1955 and 1965!

CLAUDE:
True, you haven't changed much. I wonder if it's normal for a human being to change so little in ten years.

ALEX I:
There . . . more contempt.

CLAUDE:
That's right . . . contempt. That's the word. I've gone from blind admiration to utter contempt . . . little by little, step by step . . . When you're a child and you *want* to admire someone, there's no fault, no blemish, no vice that can cloud your determination to admire . . . A hero's a hero, once and for always! It's absolute, incredibly inspiring! And nourishing! But as you get older . . . you change, of course. And you

wanted to change, to be more like him, your perfect hero who helped you through the difficulties of childhood, the problems of adolescence . . . But your hero, he stays the same, on his pedestal . . . How pathetic! Your childhood and your hero crumble at the same time. At the same time you discover the cracks in your hero and the naiveté of your childhood . . . You could die of shame . . . for having been wrong. *Silence.* You continue to grow, and you watch the cracks widen until your hero is so grotesque, you say: is that what I admired? And they say we get the heroes we deserve . . . *Silence.* I hope no one ever deserved you. *He picks up a few more sheets of paper.* I really have put all my contempt for you into this. All my . . . contempt. There's no other word. It's all there, your spinelessness, your intellectual laziness . . . your incredible intellectual laziness. You don't even know intelligence exists, that it can be used. You've never been interested in anything in your life! Or anyone. You've been totally egotistical and egocentric. It's not even a question of being mean . . . it's just unthinking selfishness . . . To be mean, you have to be conscious, use your intelligence! That's why you're so impenetrable. We can't even scratch you, others' nails don't exist for you! Your only consideration is for yourself, others can sort out their own problems . . . yours too, while they're at it. For instance, when I realized Madame Cantin in Sorel was no more important than the rest of us, and we were no more important than her and her kid, my jealousy evaporated. And God knows I was jealous . . . Hey, a second family, rivals! Thieves! Even though you were never here, I was still jealous because they stole you! Don't look at me like that, we all know about Madame Cantin, even if we never mentioned it. How's that for family solidarity . . . Well, I realized then and there how little people mean to you . . . You're totally irresponsible . . . All that matters is your beer on Saturday night, broads, a quick lay in a sleazy motel, jokes, jokes and more jokes. Papa, all you really care about is jokes! And

that is contemptible. All you've changed is your jokes. You've become a great, truly great, teller of dirty jokes, nothing more, because nothing else in life interests you. Isn't that pathetic. Not an ounce of curiosity. Not a question. Nothing. You've plied the roads of Quebec all your life, building up an absurd repertoire of dirty jokes without ever asking yourself a single question! You've raised tons of dust with generations of cars on roads that weren't yet paved, and that's all you've done with your life. How can I not crucify you with my contempt? And in my play I put all that contempt into Mama's character . . . It's Mama who tells you what I think of you because she's probably the one who's suffered most from what you've been.   *Ironically:*   I did what you'd call . . . a transfer. That's my role . . . I guess. To have others say what they're incapable of saying, and what I can't say either. But now I'm not sure. After tonight I'm not so sure. I'm not sure I have the right to become a writer. Now I'm afraid of becoming as manipulative as you. I'm afraid of becoming a joke teller like you. Of giving birth to a string of jokes that are more and more tedious, and especially, insignificant. Tear up my play if you like, Papa, set fire to it, it's full of . . .   *Silence.*   Lies. Using lies I tried to tell the truth. To a certain extent I think I succeeded. I think what I wrote is good. But what's the point. What's the point, Papa, if I can't get into your heart? What's the point if you refuse to admit you have one? Look, mine's scattered all over the place, you can trample it all you want.

He goes toward the door. He turns before going out.

CLAUDE:

If I hadn't come in that night, Papa, I know you would have raped Mariette, and that too would have become a taboo subject in this house, like Madame Cantin. We would all have been . . . accomplices, once again. If no one denounces you, what will become of all of us?

74

He goes out.

ALEX I: *Ironically.*
Don't forget to thank me. If it's true, you owe it to me,
your great writer's talent. Fucking little intellectual!
That's how you've always thought of us, eh? You and
your gang!

*ALEX I picks up a few sheets of the manuscript and
starts to burn them, one by one.*

Blackout.

University of Windsor Libraries

)ATE DUE

DATE DUE

RETURNED
MAR 0 5 1990

CPSIA information can be obtained at www.ICGtesting.com
Printed in the USA
LVOW050952171212

312006LV00004B/409/P